Taste of Ch

Tasty Gifts
• COOKBOOK •

& Inspiration for the Season

Compiled by Nanette Anderson in association with Snapdragon Group℠, Tulsa, OK.

Print ISBN 978-1-61626-835-0

eBook Editions:
Adobe Digital Edition (.epub) 978-1-62029-106-1
Kindle and MobiPocket Edition (.prc) 978-1-62029-107-8

Published by Barbour Publishing, Inc., P.O. Box 719, Uhrichsville, Ohio 44683, www.barbourbooks.com

Our mission is to publish and distribute inspirational products offering exceptional value and biblical encouragement to the masses.

Member of the
Evangelical Christian
Publishers Association

Printed in the United States of America.

Taste of Christmas

Tasty Gifts
•COOKBOOK•

& Inspiration for the Season

BARBOUR
PUBLISHING

May Peace be your gift
at Christmas and your
blessing all year through!

UNKNOWN

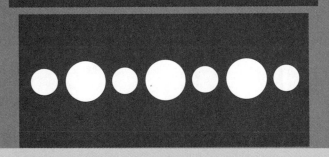

Contents

There are few gifts as affordable and well received as gifts of food—cookies, cakes, pies, breads, candies, the list goes on. Those special people on your gift list are sure to be impressed that you took the time and care to create something beautiful, warm, and delicious with your own hands, especially during the busy holiday season.

Tasty Gifts Cookbook is filled with wonderful recipes, each with an idea for turning it into a great gift for your friends and family. Why purchase one more useless trinket when you can give something special from your kitchen? Give a gift that will be remembered long after the season has passed.

When we recall Christmas past,
we usually find that the simplest
things—not the great occasions—
give off the greatest glow
of happiness.

BOB HOPE

Jams and Toppings

*A generous person will prosper;
whoever refreshes others will be refreshed.*

PROVERBS 11:25 NIV

Red Pepper Gem-Jams

4 medium fresh sweet red peppers
4 medium fresh jalapeño peppers
1 cup white vinegar

5 cups sugar
1 teaspoon red food coloring
6 ounces liquid fruit pectin

Seed and chop peppers. Put red and jalapeño peppers and white vinegar into blender and process until smooth. Put mixture in stockpot and stir in sugar. Cook over medium heat until mixture boils. Boil for 10 minutes. Remove from heat and stir in red food coloring and liquid fruit pectin. Return to heat and boil for 1 minute. Add more food coloring to make mixture bright red. Fill sterilized jars and seal with tight-fitting lids.
Yield: 8 half-pint jars.

As a Gift: Cut pepper-themed fabric circles 2 inches greater than the diameter of the jar ring. Tie fabric over lid with raffia. Attach a label identifying the jam and a greeting (*Feliz Navidad* goes well with pepper jam).

Green Pepper Gem-Jams

4 medium fresh sweet green
   peppers
4 medium fresh jalapeño peppers
1 cup white vinegar

5 cups sugar
1 teaspoon green food coloring
6 ounces liquid fruit pectin

Seed and chop peppers. Put green peppers and white vinegar into blender and process until smooth. Put mixture in stockpot and stir in sugar. Cook over medium heat until mixture boils. Boil for 10 minutes. Remove from heat and stir in green food coloring and liquid fruit pectin. Return to heat and boil for 1 minute. Add more food coloring to make mixture bright green. Fill sterilized jars with jelly and seal with tight-fitting lids.

Yield: 8 half-pint jars.

As a Gift: Cut pepper-themed fabric circles 2 inches greater than the diameter of the jar ring. Tie fabric over lid with raffia. Attach a label identifying the jam and a greeting (*Feliz Navidad* goes well with pepper jam). Give away two—one red and one green—for a festive treat!

Raspberry Jam

5 cups crushed raspberries	1 teaspoon lemon juice
7 cups sugar	Dash salt
1 box premium dry fruit pectin	1 teaspoon butter

Prepare jam according to instructions included in pectin.

Yield: 8 half-pint jars.

. . . .

As a Gift: Cut 12-inch circles of festive Christmas fabric. Place each jar in the center of a circle (pattern side down) and bring edges of the fabric up to gather tightly over the top of the jar. Tie off with coordinating ribbon to form a fabric spout. Greeting tags can be purchased in a wide array of Christmas shapes and sizes, prepunched to tie onto your gift. Or make your own by stamping and cutting out shapes from colorful thin foam sheets or card stock available at any craft store.

Hot Fudge Ice Cream Topping

8 ounces unsweetened chocolate
6 tablespoons butter
1 cup water
⅔ cup sugar

12 tablespoons corn syrup
½ teaspoon salt
2 tablespoons vanilla

In small, heavy saucepan, melt chocolate and butter slowly over low heat until combined. Meanwhile, in another saucepan, heat water to boiling. Stir melted mixture into boiling water. Add sugar, corn syrup, salt, and vanilla and mix until smooth. Turn heat up and stir until mixture boils; adjust heat. Allow sauce to boil for eight minutes, stirring occasionally. Pour very hot sauce into sterilized 8-ounce jars and seal lids tightly. Cool away from drafts. *Yield: 1 to 2 cups.*

As a Gift: Wrap a jar in tissue paper and ribbon. Place in an ice cream bowl and bundle the whole thing in clear gift wrap tied off with a wide red velvet ribbon. Tie a small ladle into the bow.

Caramel Ice Cream Topping

2 cups sugar
½ cup water
¼ cup corn syrup
¼ teaspoon salt

¾ cup room temperature
    heavy cream
3 tablespoons butter

In heavy saucepan, combine sugar, water, corn syrup, and salt. Over medium heat, bring to gentle boil until candy thermometer reads 350 degrees or mixture begins to turn golden brown. Immediately whisk in *half* of cream and butter. Whisk gently until smooth. Add rest of cream and butter and allow mixture to reheat, but *do not boil*. Cool to very warm. *Yield: 1 to 2 cups.*

As a Gift: While sauce is still liquid, pour into a pretty clear glass serving container with a lid. (Prowl antique or secondhand shops for unusual containers.) Tie a ribbon and greeting tag around the lid. You may want to include a pretty serving spoon or ladle tied into the ribbon. Keep refrigerated until you're ready to give your gift.

Jalapeño Pepper Sauce

1 medium-size jar dill pickles,
drained
1 small fresh jalapeño pepper,
chopped

⅔ cup sugar
½ teaspoon salt

Put pickles, peppers, sugar, and salt in blender and pulse until
almost smooth. Store in refrigerator for several weeks.

Yield: 1 to 2 cups.

As a Gift: Store the sauce in refrigerator in a Christmas-decorated
plastic container with tight-seal lid. Place it on an appetizer plate you
are gifting along with a block of cream cheese (in its original wrapper).
If you wish, include a small, fat appetizer knife that coordinates with
the plate. Bundle it all in clear gift wrap and tie off the top with ribbon.
Include a gift card with a serving suggestion: *Keep refrigerated!*
Pour sauce over cheese block and serve with crackers.

Easy Bread and Butter Pickles

1 (48 ounce) jar dill pickles
1 small onion, sliced
¾ cup white vinegar

2 cups sugar
1 teaspoon pickling spice

Drain pickles and refill jar with cold water. Let soak for twenty minutes and drain. Slice pickles into chunks and return them to jar. Slice small onion over pickles. Bring remaining ingredients to boil. Pour over pickles. Refrigerate for several days.

Yield: 3 pints.

As a Gift: Remove labels from the jar and add your own with the name of your gift and your greeting. Buy pretty sticky-back labels at a craft or stationery store. Cut a piece of burlap or brown wrapping paper (anything that looks rustic) into a circle 2 or 3 inches larger than the diameter of your jar lid. Place tightly over lid and tie raffia around it at the neck to secure it.

Fig Jam

5 cups fresh crushed figs
  (do not peel)
1 box dry premium fruit pectin
½ cup water

¼ cup lemon juice
½ teaspoon salt
1 tablespoon butter
6 cups sugar

In large pot, combine figs, pectin, water, lemon juice, salt, and butter. Bring to boil for one minute. Add sugar all at once, stirring gently, and bring back to boil for 1 minute. Pour into prepared canning jars and seal lids on tightly. Place jars upside down for 5 minutes, then invert and cool.

Yield: 8 half pint jars.

As a Gift: Add your own label with greeting and top jar with brown wrapping paper tied on with raffia. Present your gift in a basket lined with a holiday napkin. Include a wrapped section of a good dry cheese, like Emmentaler or parmesan, and a small package of gourmet crackers. Tie a bow to the basket handle.

Flavored Pancake Syrup

Liquid flavorings (blueberry, strawberry, etc.)
Maple syrup

Note: A wide variety of liquid flavorings are available at most culinary stores.

Stir small amount of flavoring into two cups of syrup. Taste test. Add more for stronger flavor. Store in refrigerator.

Yield: 2 cups.

As a Gift: Present your gift in small-neck slender bottles with good corks or screw-on caps. Look for these in craft or cooking stores. Tie a label and greeting around the neck of the bottle. You may want to place the syrup in a basket (line it with wood shavings or burlap or any filler you like) along with a box of pancake mix and a new pancake turner.

Pepper Dip Mix

2 tablespoons Herbes de Provence
seasoning
1 teaspoon garlic salt
½ teaspoon crushed basil flakes

½ teaspoon crushed oregano flakes
1 teaspoon dried onion flakes
1 teaspoon crushed red pepper

Combine Provence, salt, basil flakes, oregano flakes, onion flakes, and red
pepper. Mix well. Serve with toasted baguette slices.

Yield: about 1 cup.

As a Gift: Seal into small cellophane gift bag. Make your own label by
stapling a card stock tent over top of bag at closure. Include a serving
suggestion: *Mix with 1 cup good olive oil an hour before serving. Spread
onto flat plate. Cut thin baguette slices. Butter and bake to crunchy
crouton dryness on cookie sheet at 300 degrees for 1 hour.*

Peach Jam

4 cups peaches, finely chopped
2 tablespoons lemon juice
1 box premium dry fruit pectin

1 teaspoon butter
Dash salt
5½ cups sugar

In heavy saucepan, combine peaches, lemon juice, fruit pectin, butter, and salt. Bring to boil, stirring constantly for 1 minute. Add sugar all at once and bring to boil for 1 minute longer. Pour into 8-ounce canning jars. Attach lids and invert jars for 5 minutes. Jars will seal as jam cools.
Yield: 8 jars.

As a Gift: Present a jar of jam hot glued atop a fitting candle holder you are gifting. Decorate the jam lid with a raffia or Christmas ribbon. Bundle all in clear gift wrap and tie with a fabric ribbon.

Cranberry Chutney

1 (12 ounce) bag fresh or frozen
  cranberries
1 cup sugar
½ cup water
1 granny smith apple, chopped

½ teaspoon salt
2 teaspoons ground cinnamon
1 teaspoon ground ginger
¼ teaspoon ground cloves

In large saucepan, combine cranberries, sugar, water, apple, salt, and spices. Bring to boil. Reduce immediately to simmer for 20 minutes until tender, stirring constantly. Cool in pan and refrigerate.

Yield: 2 cups.

As a Gift: Present chutney in Christmas-decorated jar or sealed in plastic storage container and presented on an appetizer plate you are gifting, along with a block of gruyére cheese and gourmet crackers. Top with a bow and your greeting.

Mango Ice Cream Topping

2½ cups very ripe large variety
   mangos, peeled and chopped
1 tablespoon butter
1 tablespoon packed brown sugar

1 teaspoon lemon juice
4 tablespoons water
Dash salt

Combine all ingredients in saucepan and cook over medium heat for
10 minutes until sauce thickens, stirring constantly. Pour into prepared
canning jars and seal with canning lid. Invert jars for 5 minutes and then
turn upright. Jars will vacuum seal as they cool.
Yield: 2 cups.

As a Gift: Present in a decorated jar with a new
ice-cream scoop you are gifting.

Strawberry Waffle Topping

1 quart washed, stemmed
   strawberries
½ cup sugar

1 tablespoon butter
Dash salt

Chop half of berries and combine with sugar, butter, and salt in saucepan.
Cook on medium heat for about 10 minutes, until thickened.
Blend remaining berries until smooth. Stir berries into cooked topping
and cool. Pour into Christmas serving dish you are gifting and refrigerate.

Yield: 2 cups.

As a Gift: Present in a lined basket with a nice box of waffle
or pancake mix. Tie a thick ribbon and greeting to the handle.

Blueberry Topping

1 quart blueberries (fresh are best)
½ cup sugar
1 teaspoon lemon juice

1 tablespoon butter
Dash salt

In heavy saucepan, bring ingredients to boil. Immediately reduce heat to simmer for 10 to 12 minutes, stirring constantly until thickened. Pour into prepared canning jars and seal with canning lids. Invert jars for 5 minutes and then turn upright. Jars will vacuum seal.

Yield: 4 eight-ounce jars.

As a Gift: Present your gift in a pretty Christmas basket along with a new ice-cream scoop. You may want to include a gift certificate to a favorite ice-cream shop or coupon for a store brand.

Christmas Plum Jam

6 cups pitted, unpeeled plums
⅔ cup water
1 (1.75 ounce) box premium dry
    fruit pectin

6 cups sugar
½ teaspoon lemon juice
1 tablespoon butter
Dash salt

Place chopped plums in ⅔ cup water in saucepan and simmer for 10 minutes. Add pectin. Stir well. Bring to boil for 1 minute. Add sugar, lemon juice, butter, and salt all at once and continue stirring. Bring back to boil for 1 minute. Pour hot jam into prepared jars and screw on sealing lids. Invert for 5 minutes; set jars upright. They will seal as they cool.

Yield: 8 to 10 eight-ounce jars, or 5 pint jars.

As a Gift: On a heavy plastic disposable plate, center a labeled, decorated jar of the plum jam. Buy a small fresh pine wreath and place it around the jar for presentation. Slip your greeting card under the wreath, or tie it onto the jar lid.

Kickin' Christmas Pomegranate Sauce

1 (12 ounce) bag fresh cranberries
2 tablespoons water
1 cup sugar
Dash salt

1 tablespoon fresh ginger, grated
2 tablespoons red wine vinegar
½ cup fresh pomegranate seeds

Bring cranberries, water, sugar, salt, and ginger to simmer until cranberries pop open. Remove from heat and stir in vinegar. Let cool. Add pomegranate seeds. Serve well chilled.

Yield: 2 cups.

As a Gift: This zesty cranberry sauce is a wonderfully fresh take on the normal orange and nut flavored ones. Present your gift in a clear Christmas jar with a good lid. Decorate with a topper and tie your greeting into the ribbon or use a self-stick label on the jar. Include instruction: *Keep refrigerated.*

Cranberry Relish

1 cup boiling water
1 (1.5 ounce) package strawberry-
   flavored gelatin
1 (8 ounce) can crushed pineapple,
   drained (save the syrup)
1 (15 ounce) can prepared
   cranberry sauce

1 (8 ounce) can mandarin oranges,
   drained and chopped
½ cup nuts, chopped
½ cup finely chopped celery,
   optional
Dash salt

Stir boiling water into gelatin until dissolved. Add ½ cup pineapple syrup
(add water to make ½ cup if needed). Stir in cranberry sauce. Allow to
set just slightly in refrigerator. Then add fruit, nuts, celery, and salt.
Mix gently and store in refrigerator.

Yield: 2 cups.

As a Gift: This relish beautifully complements holiday turkey or ham.
Present your gift in a clear, lidded jar. Decorate the top only, as the
relish is such a pretty color and should show through the glass.
You might include a small relish dish with a spoon as part of your gift.

Chunky Cranberry Relish

1 pound raw cranberries
2 cups sugar
3 crisp apples, cored and chopped
(skins on)

2 oranges, peeled and chopped
1 cup walnuts, chopped
Dash salt

Cook cranberries and sugar in ½ cup water until soft, about 10 minutes.
Cool well. Then combine with apples, oranges, walnuts, and salt.
Mix well. Chill in refrigerator overnight.

Yield: 4 cups.

As a Gift: Homemade cranberry relish beats out the canned brands at the
store by a mile! Present this fresh relish in sealed plastic ware wrapped in
a pretty Christmas tea towel and tied with red velvet ribbon. Be sure to
label the relish: *Keep refrigerated and serve cold.*

Homemade Corn Relish

1 cup canned or fresh corn
1 cup cabbage
1 cup mild onion, chopped
1 cup cucumbers, chopped
½ cup fresh tomatoes, chopped
½ cup fresh red bell pepper, chopped

1 cup cider vinegar
1 cup granulated sugar
½ teaspoon celery seed
¾ teaspoon salt
½ teaspoon pepper
3 dashes turmeric

In large stew pan, combine corn, cabbage, onion, cucumbers, tomatoes, bell pepper, vinegar, sugar, celery seed, salt, pepper, and turmeric. Cook about 15 minutes. Vegetables should remain firm but not hard. Spoon into prepared pint jars and seal. Invert jars for five minutes. Place right side up to seal as they cool. Store in refrigerator.

Yield: about 4 pints.

As a gift: Cut out cheesecloth toppers and tie on with raffia at the jar neck. Label your jar, and provide a serving suggestion: *Store in refrigerator and serve as a cold side accompaniment to any meat dish!*

French Bread Spread

1 cup farmer's cheese, grated
½ cup walnuts, chopped

⅓ cup dried cranberries
2 tablespoons honey

Gently stir together cheese, walnuts, cranberries, and honey until blended.
Keep refrigerated.

Yield: 1½ cups.

As a Gift: Present this wonderful spread in a seasonal plastic storage
container atop a light cutting board you are gifting. Include the
freshest loaf of French bread you can locate.

Cakes, Pies, and Breads

Selfishness makes Christmas a burden; love makes it a delight.

UNKNOWN

Stephanie's Pumpkin Roll

¾ cup flour
1 cup sugar
3 eggs
⅔ cup canned pumpkin
2 teaspoons cinnamon
1 teaspoon baking soda

FILLING:
1 (8 ounce) package cream cheese
½ stick butter
1 cup powdered sugar
½ teaspoon vanilla

Combine flour, sugar, eggs, pumpkin, cinnamon, and baking soda. Mix well. Pour into lightly greased jelly roll pan lined with waxed paper. Bake at 350 degrees for about 15 minutes. Cool in pan 5 minutes. Flip out on tea towel dusted with powdered sugar. Peel off waxed paper. Roll and let stand ½ hour. Filling: Combine cream cheese, butter, sugar, and vanilla. Unroll dough and cover with cream cheese filling. Gently reroll and refrigerate. *Yield: 8 slices.*

As a Gift: Present your gift on a narrow, oblong Christmas plate you're gifting and bundle it in clear Christmas wrap. Tie with a bow and attach your greeting.

Chocolate Cake Baked in a Jar

2 straight-sided, wide-mouth
   canning jars with lids
1 cup flour
1 cup sugar
½ teaspoon baking soda
¼ teaspoon ground cinnamon
⅓ cup butter

¼ cup water
4 tablespoons unsweetened cocoa
   powder
¼ cup buttermilk
1 egg, beaten
¼ cup walnuts, finely chopped
½ teaspoon vanilla

Lightly grease jars. Combine flour, sugar, baking soda, and cinnamon in mixing bowl. In saucepan, combine butter, water, and cocoa, Stir over medium heat until blended. Add buttermilk, egg, nuts, and vanilla. Beat until smooth. Pour into jars, filling half full. Place them on cookie sheet and bake at 325 degrees about 40 minutes. As soon as cakes come out, screw on sealing lids. As they cool, the jars will seal. *Yield: 2 cakes.*

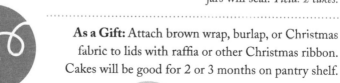

As a Gift: Attach brown wrap, burlap, or Christmas fabric to lids with raffia or other Christmas ribbon. Cakes will be good for 2 or 3 months on pantry shelf.

Pumpkin Cake Baked in a Jar

8 straight-sided, wide-mouth pint
   jars, lightly greased
⅔ cup vegetable shortening
2½ cups sugar
3 eggs
2 cups canned pumpkin
⅔ cup water

3⅓ cups flour
½ teaspoon baking powder
1½ teaspoons salt
1 teaspoon each ground cloves,
   allspice, and cinnamon
2 teaspoons baking soda
1 cup walnuts, chopped

Cream together shortening and sugar. Blend in eggs, pumpkin, and water.
Set aside. Mix together flour, baking powder, salt, spices, and baking soda.
Add to wet ingredients and gently blend. Add nuts. Pour into jars, filling
each half full. Bake on cookie sheet at 325 degrees about 40 minutes.
Apply sealing lids as soon as cakes are removed from oven. Jars will seal as
they cool. Store in pantry up to 3 months. *Yield: 8 cakes.*

As a Gift: Attach raffia ribbons to jar lids decorated with brown wrap,
burlap, or other Christmas fabric cut to fit. Label your jars and include a
serving suggestion: *Slice and serve warm with ice cream or whipped cream.*

Applesauce Cake Baked in a Jar

8 straight-sided, wide-mouth
    canning jars, lightly greased
2½ cups sugar
⅔ cup shortening
3 eggs
3 cups flour
1 teaspoon cinnamon

2 teaspoons baking soda
1½ teaspoons salt
⅔ cup water
2 cups applesauce
⅓ cup raisins
⅔ cup walnuts, chopped

Cream together sugar, shortening, and eggs. Set aside. Combine flour, cinnamon, baking soda, and salt. Add to shortening mixture. Add water, applesauce, raisins, and walnuts. Gently stir until well blended. Pour into lightly greased jars, filling half full. Bake on cookie sheet at 325 degrees for 45 minutes. Apply lids as soon as cakes come out of oven. The jars will seal as they cool. *Yield: 8 cakes.*

As a Gift: Decorate jar lids with brown wrap, burlap, or other Christmas fabric. Tie on your greeting with raffia or ribbon. Don't forget to label your jars! Cakes will stay fresh for 3 or 4 months.

Lemon Bundt Cake

3 eggs   1 white cake mix
1 (16 ounce) can lemon pie filling

Whisk eggs and pie filling together. Add cake mix and blend well. Pour into greased bundt cake pan and bake at 350 degrees for 45 minutes. Serve with whipped cream. *Yield: 12 to 14 slices.*

As a Gift: Place the cake on a cake dish you are gifting and bundle in clear kitchen wrap around—try one of the red or green cellophane wraps available at the holidays. (Be sure to buy the extra wide roll for these bigger wrapping projects.) Lay the wrap over the cake and bring edges under plate and secure. Gently attach a bow or ribbon.

Christmas Rum Bundt Cake

1 yellow cake mix
¼ cup flour
1 teaspoon salt
1 (4 ounce) box instant vanilla
   pudding mix
4 eggs, beaten
½ cup water
½ cup vegetable oil

½ cup rum or 1 teaspoon rum
   flavoring
½ cup walnuts, finely chopped
GLAZE:
½ stick butter
¼ cup water
1 cup sugar
½ cup rum

Combine cake mix, flour, salt, and pudding mix. Combine eggs, water, oil, and rum flavoring. Add to dry mixture. Spread nuts on bottom of greased bundt cake pan. Pour in batter. Bake at 350 degrees for 1 hour. Cool. Glaze: In saucepan, combine butter, water, sugar, and rum. Boil for 5 minutes. Cool slightly and pour over cake. (Note: Alcohol is rendered harmless during cooking. Only the flavor remains.) *Yield: 12 to 14 slices.*

As a Gift: Dot the crown of the cake with maraschino cherries. Dust with powdered sugar. Wrap with cellophane wrap and present with your greeting and label.

Pineapple Upside Down Cake

1 box supermoist yellow cake mix
1 (20 ounce) can pineapple slices in
   juice, drained, juice reserved
¼ cup butter or margarine

1 cup packed brown sugar
1 (6 ounce) jar maraschino cherries
   without stems, drained

Prepare cake batter according to package instructions, substituting drained pineapple juice for water in recipe. Melt butter in 9x13-inch baking pan. Sprinkle brown sugar evenly over butter. Arrange pineapple slices in single layer, placing a cherry in center of each. Pour batter over all and bake at 350 degrees for 45 minutes. Remove from oven and immediately run knife around edges of cake to loosen. Place foil-covered, appropriately-sized piece of heavy cardboard over cake and invert. Let sit 5 minutes before removing baking pan. Cool.

Yield: 12 to 14 slices.

As a Gift: The foil-covered cardboard will serve as a festive plate. Bundle all in cellophane wrapping paper and tie with a Christmas bow. Include a serving suggestion: *Serve warm with whipped cream.*

Festive Raspberry Pie

5 cups whole fresh raspberries
1 teaspoon lemon juice
1½ cups sugar
2 tablespoons quick-cooking
   tapioca

2 tablespoons cornstarch
½ teaspoon salt
2 (9 inch) pastry crusts, unbaked

Gently rinse and let raspberries drain well. Arrange them in unbaked pastry crust. Sprinkle lemon juice over berries. Combine sugar, tapioca, cornstarch, and salt. Pour evenly over berries. Dot with butter and seal second crust over top. Make a few slits to allow for steam venting as pie cooks. Bake at 350 degrees for about 45 minutes or until lightly brown and bubbly.

Yield: 8 slices.

As a Gift: A pretty pie plate makes a wonderful gift. Bake your pie in one for presentation. This pie is *always* welcomed because it is rarely made. If nice fresh raspberries cannot be found, use frozen. (Freeze berries in late summer when they are inexpensive to purchase.)

Yule-Time Caramel Pie

2 cups whole milk
1 cup packed brown sugar
2 tablespoons butter
⅓ cup flour

½ teaspoon salt
2 beaten egg yolks
½ teaspoon vanilla
1 (9 inch) pastry shell, unbaked

Heat milk on medium heat in heavy saucepan. Add sugar and butter. Stir enough water into flour to make loose paste. Whisk into milk along with salt and cook until thickened. Add eggs yolks, stirring constantly for two more minutes. Stir in vanilla and pour into unbaked pastry shell. Bake at 350 degrees for about 15 minutes or until golden brown.

Yield: 10 slices.

As a Gift: This custard pie will be a welcome gift on any holiday occasion! It's very rich, so it goes a long way. Present it in a pie plate you'd like to gift, or give it with a pretty pie server with a ribbon tied to the handle.

Kris Kringle's Pumpkin Pie

1 (15 ounce) can pumpkin
⅔ cup sugar
½ teaspoon salt
1 teaspoon ground cinnamon
½ teaspoon ground ginger

½ teaspoon ground cloves
3 medium eggs, beaten
1 (12 ounce) can evaporated milk
1 (9 inch) pastry shell, unbaked

In mixing bowl, combine pumpkin, sugar, salt, and spices. Whisk in eggs and evaporated milk. Pour into unbaked pastry shell and bake at 400 degrees for 15 minutes. Then reduce heat to 325 degrees for 45 minutes. Pie is done when clean, dry knife is inserted in middle and comes out clean.

Yield: 8 slices.

As a Gift: Pumpkin pie isn't just for Thanksgiving anymore! Present it bundled in cellophane wrap and tied with a Christmas bow! Include a gift certificate for a ready-made pie from one of the local bakeries or restaurants.

Holiday Pecan Pie

1 tablespoon flour
¼ cup sugar
2 dashes salt
3 eggs, beaten
1 cup dark corn syrup

¼ cup water
2 tablespoons melted butter
¾ cup pecans, chopped, or 1 cup halved
1 (9 inch) pastry shell, unbaked

Combine flour, sugar, and salt. Whisk together eggs, corn syrup, and water. Add to dry mixture. Add melted butter and chopped nuts. Pour into unbaked pastry shell and bake at 425 degrees for 10 minutes, then reduce oven to 350 degrees and bake 30 minutes longer.
Yield: 8 slices.

As a Gift: This pie will make you famous! People just can't believe you'd actually give them a homemade pecan pie! Present your pie atop a pretty set of round holiday placemats. Bundle it all in cellophane wrap and tie with a bow.

Santa's Favorite Apple Pie

5 or 6 granny smith apples, peeled,
   cored and thin sliced
½ cup packed brown sugar
½ cup sugar
1 teaspoon lemon juice
1 tablespoon flour
½ teaspoon cinnamon

2 tablespoons red hot cinnamon
   candies
½ teaspoon nutmeg
½ teaspoon salt
¼ stick of butter, cut up
1 tablespoon red hots
2 (9 inch) pastry crusts, unbaked

Mix together apples, sugars, lemon juice, flour, cinnamon, candies,
nutmeg, and salt. Pour into unbaked pastry crust. Dot generously
with butter and red hot candies. Top with second crust
and bake at 350 degrees for 50 minutes.

Yield: 8 slices.

As a Gift: If you are not giving the pie plate as a gift, bake your
pie in a disposable tin. Include a pretty Christmas pie
server or new rolling pin tied with a bow.

Christmas Wonder Cherry Pie

3 cups pitted sour cherries (do *not* use cherry pie filling)
1 cup sugar
1 teaspoon lemon juice
3 tablespoons minute tapioca
½ teaspoon salt
¼ teaspoon almond extract
2 (9 inch) piecrusts, unbaked
¼ stick of butter, cut up

Mix together cherries, sugar, lemon juice, tapioca, salt, and almond extract. Pour into unbaked pastry crust. Dot generously with butter. Top with second crust and bake at 350 degrees for 50 minutes.
Yield: 8 slices.

As a Gift: Present this classic Christmas pie along with a stack of clear dessert plates. These are extremely handy all year long. They work well for Christmas because they coordinate with any china.

Banana Cream Pie

¾ cup sugar
2½ teaspoons cornstarch
½ teaspoon salt
2 cups whole milk
2 egg yolks

1 teaspoon vanilla
2 tablespoons butter
2 cups thinly sliced bananas
1 (9 inch) homemade or ready-
    made pastry shell, baked

Combine sugar, cornstarch, and salt in large heavy saucepan. Whisk in milk and egg yolks. Cook, stirring constantly until thickened. Stir in vanilla and butter and allow to cool very slightly. Meanwhile, arrange banana slices in baked and cooled crust. Pour custard evenly over all and refrigerate. Top with whipped cream when cool.

Yield: 8 slices.

As a Gift: Present your pie seated on a pretty hostess plate you're gifting. Bundle all in cellophane wrap and tie with a bow. Be sure the recipient refrigerates immediately until serving time.

Lisa's Easy Christmas Kranz

1 loaf frozen white dough
1 stick butter, softened
1 cup packed brown sugar
½ cup maraschino cherries,
   chopped
1 cup pecans, chopped
Salt

FROSTING:
1 cup powdered sugar
½ stick butter
Dash salt
½ teaspoon vanilla
Milk

Thaw frozen dough in plastic bag at room temperature until soft but not rising. Roll out into thin oblong rectangle. Spread butter, then top with brown sugar. Sprinkle with cherries and pecans. Very lightly salt. Roll tightly from long edge. Pinch ends to seal and bring ends together on greased cookie sheet to form circle. Cover with damp light towel and allow to rise for about 1 hour. Bake at 375 degrees for about 30 minutes. Frosting: Combine sugar, butter, salt, and vanilla with enough milk to make a good consistency. When almost cool, brush on frosting. *Yield: 12 slices.*

As a Gift: Present your gift on a Christmas cake plate that you are gifting. Cover with clear plastic wrap and garnish with a bow. Tie a holiday cake server into the bow.

Old-Fashioned Gingerbread

½ cup shortening
½ cup sugar
1 egg
1 cup molasses
2½ cups flour
½ teaspoon salt

½ teaspoon baking soda
¾ teaspoon baking powder
1½ teaspoons ground ginger
1 teaspoon cinnamon
1 cup hot water
Powdered sugar

Cream together shortening, sugar, egg, and molasses. Set aside. Combine flour, salt, baking soda, baking powder, ginger, and cinnamon. Add to wet mixture. Stir in hot water and mix well. Pour into greased and floured 8x10-inch baking dish and bake at 350 degrees for 30 to 40 minutes. Sprinkle lightly with powdered sugar when cool. *Yield: 10 to 12 slices.*

As a Gift: Bake the gingerbread in a Christmas baking dish you are gifting. This size baking dish is very handy for year-round use, so make sure it isn't too Christmassy. Label with a serving suggestion: *Serve warm with whipped cream.*

Sugar and Spice Cupcakes

½ cup shortening
1 cup packed brown sugar
1 cup sugar
2 eggs
2 cups flour
½ teaspoon salt
½ teaspoon baking soda
½ teaspoon baking powder

1 teaspoon cinnamon
½ teaspoon cloves
½ teaspoon nutmeg
½ teaspoon lemon juice
1 cup milk
1 (16 ounce) can buttercream frosting
Colored sprinkles

Cream shortening and sugars until well blended. Add eggs and mix well. Set aside. Combine flour, salt, baking soda, baking powder, and spices. Mix lemon juice into milk to sour it. Into creamed mixture, alternate portions of dry mixture and milk, mixing well after each. Pour into muffin tin lined with cupcake papers. Fill each paper only ⅔ full. Bake at 375 degrees for 20 minutes. Cool, frost, and add sprinkles. *Yield: 2 dozen.*

As a Gift: Arrange the cupcakes on a paper-doily-lined Christmas hostess plate you are gifting. Bundle all with cellophane wrap and tie with a bow.

Individual Peach Cobblers

½ stick butter
1 cup flour
1 cup sugar

1 teaspoon baking powder
¾ cup milk
2 cups sliced peaches

Melt butter in 4 ramekins, 1 tablespoon each. Combine flour, sugar, baking powder, milk and mix into batter. Pour evenly over butter in ramekins. Do not stir. Place ½ cup peaches atop batter and place ramekins on cookie sheet. Bake at 350 degrees for about 40 minutes.

Yield: 4 individual cobblers.

As a Gift: Bundle cobblers in clear gift cellophane wrap and tie up with a bow. Include a suggestion to serve slightly warm topped with vanilla ice cream. The ramekins are part of the gift!

Happy Holidays Banana Cake

½ cup shortening
1 cup sugar
2 eggs
½ teaspoon vanilla
2¼ cups flour
½ teaspoon salt

⅔ teaspoon baking soda
½ teaspoon lemon juice
½ cup sour milk or buttermilk
3 very ripe (black) bananas, pulped
1 (16 ounce) can buttercream frosting

Cream together shortening and sugar. Add beaten eggs and vanilla. Set aside. Combine flour, salt, and baking soda. Mix lemon juice into milk to sour it. Into creamed mixture, alternate portions of dry mixture and milk, mixing well after each. Fold in bananas. Bake in 8x11-inch glass baking dish at 350 degrees for 30 minutes. Cool well and frost with buttercream frosting. *Yield: 14 to 16 squares.*

As a Gift: This wonderfully moist and tender cake makes a great gift. Bake it right in a new baking dish you'd like to gift. Bundle all in cellophane wrap and include a personal, handwritten greeting.

Fruity Cranberry Crisp

1 (16 ounce) bag cranberries,
   cooked
½ cup maple syrup
2 granny smith apples, peeled
   and sliced
2 ripe pears, peeled and cubed
1 teaspoon lemon juice
½ teaspoon cinnamon
½ teaspoon nutmeg

½ teaspoon cloves
½ teaspoon ginger
STREUSEL:
¼ cup walnuts, chopped
1 cup quick-cooking oatmeal
¼ cup flour
¼ cup packed brown sugar
¼ stick butter, cut up

Drain any excess water off cranberries after cooking and add maple syrup.
Stir and set aside. Gently toss apples and pears in lemon juice and spices
and arrange in 8x8-inch baking dish. Pour cranberries over all. Streusel:
Mix walnuts, oatmeal, flour, and brown sugar. Pour over top. Dot all with
butter and bake at 350 degrees for 35 to 40 minutes. *Yield: 8 servings.*

As a Gift: Present your gift baked in a new baking dish you're gifting, or
accompanied by a half-gallon of high-quality vanilla ice cream. Include
serving suggestion on your gift tag: *Serve warm topped with ice cream!*

Christmas Joy Cupcakes

1 cake mix (any flavor)
1 (16 ounce) can frosting
Colored sugar

Sprinkles
Jelly Beans

Prepare cake according to package instructions. Fill cupcake papers placed in muffin tin ⅔ full and bake. Frost and decorate.

Yield: 12 cupcakes.

As a Gift: Present cupcakes in a shallow Christmas box lined with tissue paper to keep cupcakes firmly upright. This is a great gift for a big family. . .kids love cupcakes!

Banana Bread

½ cup butter	½ teaspoon salt
1 cup sugar	3 very ripe (black) bananas
2 eggs	½ cup whole milk
2 cups flour	1 teaspoon vanilla
1 teaspoon baking soda	

Cream together butter, sugar, and eggs. Mix together flour, baking soda, and salt. Add to creamed mixture. Add bananas, milk, and vanilla. Blend well and pour into greased loaf pan. Bake at 350 degrees for about 1 hour.

Yield: 1 loaf.

As a Gift: Wrap the bread first in waxed paper and then in foil. A bow or ribbon tied around it is sufficient. You may want to place the bread in a basket along with a pretty set of small paper Christmas napkins—entertainers go through a lot of these during the holidays! Garnish with a small bunch of bananas if your basket is roomy enough.

Zucchini Bread

1 cup cooking oil
3 eggs
1 teaspoon vanilla
2 cups flour
2 cups sugar
1 tablespoon cinnamon
2 teaspoons baking soda

¼ teaspoon baking powder
1 teaspoon salt
2 cups unpeeled zucchini, coarsely
   grated and packed down
½ cup raisins
½ cup walnuts, chopped

Combine oil, eggs, and vanilla. Set aside. Combine flour, sugar, cinnamon, baking soda, baking powder, and salt. Add to wet ingredients. Mix well. Fold in zucchini, raisins, and walnuts. Mix well. Bake in 2 greased and floured loaf pans at 350 degrees for 1 hour.

Yield: 2 loaves.

As a Gift: Wrap each loaf of cooled bread first in waxed paper and then in foil. Tie velvet ribbons around each and arrange in a green tissue-lined box among a pretty set of Christmas tree ornaments.

Pumpkin Bread

1½ cups sugar	1½ cups flour
2 eggs	1 teaspoon baking soda
½ cup vegetable oil	½ teaspoon baking powder
1 cup canned pumpkin	½ teaspoon salt
¼ cup water	½ teaspoon pumpkin pie spice

Cream together sugar, eggs, oil, pumpkin, and water. Set aside. Mix together flour, baking soda, baking powder, salt, and spice. Combine with wet mixture and mix well. Spoon into lightly greased and floured loaf pan and bake at 350 degrees for about an hour.

Yield: 1 loaf.

As a Gift: Wrap the bread first in waxed paper and then in foil. Present your gift in an open, lined Christmas basket and include a pretty tablecloth or Christmas table runner. Tie an outrageously big ribbon on the basket handle!

Cranberry Bread

2 cups flour
½ teaspoon salt
1½ teaspoons baking powder
1 cup sugar
2 teaspoons baking soda
2 tablespoons hot water

1 egg, beaten
1 tablespoon butter, melted
½ cup orange juice
1 cup cooked cranberries,
   canned is fine
1 cup nuts, chopped

Combine flour, salt, baking powder, and sugar, leaving a well in the center.
Dissolve baking soda in hot water and add it along with egg, butter, and
orange juice. Blend well. Add cranberries and nuts. Pour into 2 lightly
greased and floured loaf pans. Bake at 350 degrees for 1 hour.
Yield: 2 loaves.

As a Gift: Wrap cooled loaves first in waxed paper and then in foil. Put
a Christmas bow on each. Present your gift on a serving tray you are
gifting. Line the tray with a pretty Christmas runner and include a new
bread knife.

Date Bread

¼ cup shortening	1½ teaspoons baking soda
¾ cup boiling water	2 eggs
1 cup dates, chopped	1 cup sugar
¾ cup nuts, chopped	1½ cups flour
½ teaspoon salt	½ teaspoon vanilla

Melt shortening in boiling water and pour over dates, nuts, salt, and baking soda. Let sit for 15 minutes. Add eggs, sugar, flour, and vanilla. Mix well. Pour into lightly greased and floured loaf pan. Bake at 350 degrees for 1 hour.

Yield: 1 large loaf.

As a gift: Wrap loaf first in waxed paper and then in foil. With raffia or other Christmas ribbon, tie a bow around the loaf. Line a bread basket with a set of red or green cloth napkins and place the bread inside.

Cinnamon Swirl Bread

1 loaf frozen bread dough
1 stick butter, softened
1 cup packed brown sugar
2 teaspoons cinnamon

¼ teaspoon salt
½ cup nuts, chopped
¼ cup raisins

Allow frozen dough to thaw but not rise. Roll out into short oblong; this bread will end up being baked in a loaf pan, so size is important when rolling out dough. Spread butter over all. Mix brown sugar, cinnamon, and salt. Sprinkle over butter. Sprinkle on nuts and raisins. Roll dough tightly from one short end to other. Place in large, greased loaf pan and let rise, about an hour. Bake at 350 for about 30 minutes. *Yield: 1 large loaf.*

As a Gift: When bread is cool, wrap first in waxed paper and then in foil. Place the bread in a lined box and surround it with an assortment of jarred baking spices: cinnamon, nutmeg, cloves, ginger, cinnamon sticks, whatever you like!

Lemon Poppy Seed Bread

2¼ cups flour
1¼ cups sugar
¾ cup milk
1 stick real butter, softened
3 eggs
2 tablespoons poppy seeds
1½ teaspoons baking powder
½ teaspoon lemon flavoring

1 tablespoon grated lemon peel
1 teaspoon salt
GLAZE:
⅓ cup powdered sugar
4 tablespoons butter, melted
1½ teaspoons lemon juice
Dash salt

Combine flour, sugar, milk, butter, eggs, poppy seeds, baking powder, flavoring, lemon peel, and salt. Beat on medium speed 2 to 3 minutes. Pour into greased and floured loaf pan. Bake at 350 degrees for 1 hour. Glaze: Combine sugar, butter, lemon juice, and salt. Stir. Pour glaze over bread while still warm. *Yield: 1 loaf.*

As a Gift: When very cool, wrap the bread first in waxed paper and then in foil. Present on a lightweight, wooden cutting board you are gifting. Tie a red velvet ribbon across ends and sides and make a bow. Add the recipe on your greeting tag.

Em's Rusks

4 cups self-rising flour
1 cup flaked coconut
2 cups wheat bran
1 cup salted sunflower seeds
¼ cup sunflower oil

3 teaspoons baking powder
1 teaspoon salt
4 cups buttermilk
1 pound (four sticks) margarine
1 cup honey

In large bowl, mix together flour, coconut, wheat bran, sunflower seeds, oil, baking powder, salt, buttermilk, margarine, and honey. Spoon dough into greased and floured loaf pans. Bake at 350 degrees for 1 hour. When cool, cut bread into slices and place them on cookie sheets. Slice each slab into 4 pieces, like fingerlings. Let bread dry out overnight (about 12 hours) in 200 degree low oven. *Yield: about 100 crunchy pieces.*

As a Gift: This classic South African tea bread is very healthy and just sweet enough to complement any hot drink. Place dried fingerlings like dominoes in a quality lidded Christmas tin that you will gift. Line it with waxed paper at the bottom and between each layer. Be sure to include a label such as: *Rusks: delicious South African tea crisps.*

Christmas Morning Cinnamon Rolls

1 loaf frozen bread dough	2 teaspoons cinnamon
1 stick butter, melted	½ cup walnuts, chopped
1 cup packed brown sugar	½ cup sweetened dried cranberries

Thaw frozen dough, but do not allow to rise. Roll out into thin oblong rectangle. Spread butter and top with sugar, cinnamon, walnuts, and cranberries. Roll tightly, beginning on long edge. Pinch along seam to seal. Cut into 12 slices and place in lightly greased oblong baking pan. Let rise covered with waxed paper for about an hour. Bake at 350 degrees for about 20 minutes. Don't overbake. Upon removing from oven, invert pan and dump immediately onto waxed paper to cool. *Yield: 1 dozen rolls.*

As a Gift: Plan to bake these rolls the same day you are giving them. Wrap the whole oblong of connected rolls first in waxed paper and then in foil. Present your gift in a pretty basket lined with a tea towel. If you like, include a container of whipped butter.

Christmas Pound Cake

1¼ cups butter
2½ cups sugar
5 eggs
1 teaspoon vanilla

3 cups flour
1 teaspoon baking powder
½ teaspoon salt
1 cup evaporated milk

Measure butter, sugar, eggs, and vanilla into large bowl. Blend 1 minute on low. Beat on high speed for 5 minutes, scraping sides occasionally. On low speed, mix in flour, baking powder, and salt alternately with milk. Pour into lightly greased and floured bundt pan. Bake at 350 degrees for 70 to 80 minutes. Cool in the pan for 20 minutes before removing.

As a Gift: Pound cake is perfect as a Christmas gift because it retains its moisture longer and can be served simply or dressed up with fruit and whipped cream. Any hostess on your list will appreciate receiving it! Wrap it well in colored plastic kitchen wrap and topped with a bow or presented on a pretty plate you are gifting.

Cake Pops

1 cake mix (any flavor)	½ cup vegetable oil
1 (4 ounce) box instant pudding mix (dry)	½ cup frosting (any flavor)
	6-inch cookie sticks
4 eggs	1 bag chocolate candy, melted
¾ cup water	

Combine cake mix, pudding mix, eggs, water, and oil. Beat on medium speed for two minutes. Pour into greased and floured 9x13-inch pan. Bake at 350 degrees for 30 minutes. After cake is cool, use fingers to reduce cake to coarse crumble. Mix in frosting and compact into two-inch balls. Place on a waxed-paper covered cookie sheet. Refrigerate. Dip sticks in melted chocolate and insert into cookie balls. Coat each pop with melted candy chocolate and stand in a heavy mug until set. *Yield: 15 to 20 pops.*

As a Gift: These fun cake pops make a great gift for children on your list, but adults love them, too. Bundle them together with Christmas ribbon or present them in a flower pot you'd like to gift. Put florist foam in the pot and just let the pops stand in it like blooms!

Apricot Sour Cream Coffee Cake

¾ cup butter

1½ cups packed brown sugar

2 eggs

1 teaspoon vanilla

2¼ cups flour

2 teaspoon baking powder

½ teaspoon baking soda

½ teaspoon salt

½ teaspoon cinnamon

1 cup sour cream

1½ cups dried apricots

½ cup pecans, chopped

2 tablespoons packed brown sugar

1 teaspoon cinnamon

Cream together butter, sugar, eggs, and vanilla. Combine flour, baking powder, baking soda, salt, cinnamon, and apricots. Blend this mixture into wet mixture along with sour cream. Grease and lightly flour bundt pan. Mix together pecans, sugar, and cinnamon and line bottom of pan. Spoon in batter and bake at 350 degrees for 45 minutes.

Yield: 12 to 14 slices.

As a Gift: Present your gift wrapped in plastic kitchen wrap and place a large bow on top. Include a new set of pot holders with the cake.

Mrs. Santa's Easy Cheesecake

CRUST:
1¾ cups graham cracker crumbs
1 tablespoon flour
1 stick butter, melted
⅓ cup sugar
FILLING:
12 ounces cream cheese
½ cup sugar
2 eggs

¼ teaspoon salt
TOPPING:
1½ cups sour cream
¼ cup sugar
1 teaspoon vanilla
2 or 3 (16 ounce) cans prepared
    pie fillings (various flavors)
Pint of fresh strawberries, optional

Mix together graham cracker crumbs, flour, butter, and sugar. In lightly greased pie plate, press to form crust. Beat together cream cheese, sugar, eggs, and salt. Pour into crust and bake at 375 for 25 to 30 minutes. Meanwhile, mix together sour cream, sugar, and vanilla. Spread on cheesecake after it is baked. Bake 5 to 10 minutes more. Cool and refrigerate. *Yield: 10 slices.*

As a gift: If you're giving a pie plate as your gift, prepare the cheesecake right in it. Surround it with wrapped cans of pie fillings.

Fudge Pie

¼ cup butter
¾ cup packed brown sugar
3 eggs
1 (8 ounce) package semisweet
  baking chocolate, melted
1 teaspoon vanilla

2 teaspoons strong instant coffee
  granules
¼ cup flour
1 cup walnuts, chopped
1 (9 inch) pastry shell, unbaked
½ cup walnut halves

Soften butter and combine with brown sugar. Beat until fluffy. Add eggs and mix well. Add melted chocolate, vanilla, and coffee. Mix well. Stir in flour and chopped nuts. Pour into unbaked pastry shell. Dot with walnut halves and bake at 375 for 25 to 30 minutes. Refrigerate to set.

Yield: 8 to 10 slices.

As a Gift: Bundle into clear Christmas wrap and tie with a velvet bow. Attach a pretty pie server you are gifting or a beautiful Christmas tree ornament.

Orange Pumpkin Muffins

2 eggs, beaten
½ cup sugar
¼ cup oil
½ cup orange juice
1 cup canned pumpkin
2 tablespoons grated orange rind
2 cups flour

1 tablespoon baking powder
½ teaspoon baking soda
½ teaspoon salt
¼ teaspoon each of cinnamon,
  nutmeg, and allspice
½ cup raisins
½ cup walnuts, chopped

Beat together eggs, sugar, oil, juice, pumpkin, and orange rind. Combine flour, baking powder, baking soda, salt, spices, and raisins. Add to wet mixture. Spoon batter into greased muffin tins and bake at 350 degrees for 20 minutes.

Yield: 1 dozen muffins.

As a Gift: Arrange muffins around a small tub of whipped butter on a gift plate and bundle all in cellophane wrap tied with a colorful ribbon at the top.

Streusel Coffee Cake

¾ cup sugar
⅓ cup vegetable oil
1 egg
½ cup milk
1½ cups flour
2 teaspoons baking powder
½ teaspoon salt

TOPPING:
½ cup packed brown sugar
1½ tablespoons flour
1½ teaspoons cinnamon
2 tablespoons butter
½ cup nuts, chopped

Combine sugar, oil, and egg. Add milk and beat thoroughly. Combine flour, baking powder, and salt. Stir into first mixture. Beat till smooth and spread in 9-inch square baking pan. Topping: Mix together sugar, flour, cinnamon, butter, and nuts. Sprinkle cake with topping. Bake at 375 degrees for 30 minutes.

As a Gift: A wonderful gift cake at the holidays. Great for breakfast or with coffee when friends drop in! Present it with a package of paper Christmas napkins or baked in a casserole dish you'd like to gift. Add a written prayer such as: *Heavenly Father, bless our friends with good health in the coming year.*

Cranberry Squares

3 cups flour	1 teaspoon cinnamon
¾ cup packed brown sugar	1 teaspoon salt
1 cup shortening	2 cups whole cranberries
1 stick butter	½ cup sugar
1 cup quick-cooking oats	1 cup water

Combine flour, brown sugar, shortening, butter, oats, cinnamon, and salt. Mix until crumbly and press half into 9x13-inch baking pan. Cook cranberries in sugar and water until soft, about 20 minutes. Puree in blender and pour over crust. Add remainder of crumbly mixture and bake at 350 degrees until bubbly. Cool and cut into squares.

Yield: 12 squares.

As a Gift: These rich, layered Christmas treats look so pretty on an elevated plate. You can buy stem plates for very little at discount stores, or scour your local secondhand shops for them. They make great gifts!

Soft Pretzels

1 cup water
3 cups bread flour
1 teaspoon dry milk powder
2 tablespoons sugar
1 teaspoon salt

1 tablespoon shortening
1½ teaspoons active dry yeast
1 egg white, beaten until frothy
Coarse salt

Mix together water, flour, milk powder, sugar, salt, shortening, and yeast.
Roll into ½-inch thick rectangle. Divide dough into 16 pieces and roll
each into ball. Let rise 20 minutes in a warm place. Roll each piece into
rope and shape like pretzel on greased cookie sheet. Cover and let rise 30
to 45 minutes. Brush with egg white, sprinkle with coarse salt, and bake
at 375 degrees until golden brown. *Yield: 16 pretzels.*

As a Gift: Stack these cooled pretzels upright in a
pretty, lined bread or cracker basket you are gifting.
Include 6x6-inch squares of red tissue paper or a
small pack of red tea napkins. Bundle it all in red
or green cellophane wrap and tie with a bow.

Beverages and Candy

O taste and see that the LORD is good:
blessed is the man that trusteth in him.

PSALM 34:8

Candy Cups

1 pound high quality milk
    chocolate
1 pound high quality dark
    chocolate

1 pound high quality white
    chocolate
Nuts, dried fruit, or peppermint
    stick

Break up chocolate and place each kind separately in deep bowls or glass
measuring cups with pouring spouts. Set down in gently simmering
shallow pan of water. Allow chocolate to melt slowly, stirring occasionally
with rubber spatula. When melted and smooth, pour into mini muffin
tins lined with candy papers. Fill only half full. Place a nut, small piece
of dried fruit, or sliver of peppermint stick atop each
before chocolate hardens.

Yield: 3 pounds.

As a Gift: Present your gift in the paper wrappers and nestled into small
Christmas boxes or tins with lids. You can buy these already decorated—
no wrapping required. Tie it up with a decadently beautiful bow! Recipe
makes enough for 3 gifts!

Caramel Corn

2 cups packed light brown sugar
½ cup light corn syrup
2 sticks butter
¼ teaspoon cream of tartar

1 teaspoon salt
1 teaspoon baking soda
6 quarts freshly popped corn

In large saucepan, combine sugar, corn syrup, butter, cream of tartar, and salt. Heat until boiling, stirring constantly over medium heat. Bring to rapid boil for 5 minutes. Stir in baking soda and pour over popped corn in large bowl, stirring gently until corn is coated. Spread onto cookie sheets and bake at 200 degrees for one hour, stirring 2 or 3 times during baking. Turn out onto waxed paper to cool.

Yield. 6 quarts.

As a Gift: Bag the corn in three separate large plastic bags. Create a tented label for your greeting out of card stock that is as wide as the bag. Staple or hot-glue it over the end.

Pecan Pralines

3 cups sugar
1 cup milk
2 tablespoons light corn syrup
1 teaspoon vanilla

1 tablespoon butter
½ teaspoon salt
3 cups pecan halves

In large saucepan, cook sugar, milk, and corn syrup to soft ball stage. Add vanilla, butter, salt, and pecans. Remove from heat and stir until mixture begins to thicken and starts to turn slightly opaque. Quickly drop by teaspoonfuls onto waxed paper. You will have to work fast, as these set up very quickly!

Yield: 25 to 30 pralines.

As a Gift: Line a gift tin with waxed paper and stack the pralines with waxed paper between layers. Pack the candy snugly so it doesn't shift around and break.

Almond Coconut Clusters

2 cups sugar	1 cup sliced, toasted almonds
½ cup milk	1 teaspoon vanilla
1 tablespoon light corn syrup	1 teaspoon butter
1 cup unsweetened flaked coconut	Dash salt

In heavy saucepan, combine sugar, milk, and corn syrup. Cook to soft ball stage and remove from heat. Add coconut, almonds, vanilla, butter, and salt. Stir well until mixture starts to thicken. Drop by clusters onto waxed paper, working quickly as these set up fast.

Yield: about 2 dozen.

As a Gift: Place each cluster into candy or small muffin papers with a holiday design. Line a lidded gift box or tin in a single layer. Slip a handwritten note under the lid.

Chocolate-Dipped Candy Canes

1 bag semisweet or milk
   chocolate chips

20 large candy canes, unwrapped

Melt chocolate chips in deep bowl set down in gently simmering water.
Do not let water splash into chocolate. When melted, dip base of each
cane until coated about halfway up. Hang canes from their hooks
over edge of tall bowl to allow chocolate to harden.

Yield: 20 candy canes.

. . . .

As a Gift: Present the candy canes by 4s or 5s in long cellophane gift bags
gathered at the top and tied with ribbon. Or fold the bag tops and create
your own tent label and staple it on. Make two hole punches in the label
and bring a ribbon through it from back to front where it can be tied
into a bow. You will have enough to make 4 or 5 gifts.

Chocolate-Dipped Pretzels

2 dozen large stick or twisted
thick pretzels

1 bag white, semisweet,
or milk chocolate chips

Melt chocolate chips in deep bowl set in gently simmering water.
Do not let water splash into chocolate. When chocolate is completely
melted, dip base of each pretzel until coated about halfway up.
Lay each pretzel on waxed paper to harden.

Yield: 2 dozen pretzels.

As a Gift: Present your gift in fat cellophane gift bags (look for
them in cooking and craft stores), sized to fit your
pretzels. Bunch the top with ribbon or make a tent
label and staple or hot glue it to the top of the bag.

Chocolate-Dipped Dried Apricots

2 dozen whole dried apricots   1 bag white, semisweet,
                                       or milk chocolate chips

Melt chocolate chips in deep bowl set in gently simmering water.
Do not let water splash into chocolate. When chocolate is melted,
dip base of each apricot until coated about halfway up. Lay each
apricot on waxed paper to harden.
Yield: 2 dozen.

As a Gift: Place 2 or 3 apricots into candy papers and tuck them into a
box around your gift of a pair of gloves or a nice winter scarf.
Cover with a layer of tissue paper.

Russian Tea

2 cups sweetened dry orange
    drink mix
1 envelope unsweetened dry
    lemonade
½ cup sugar

½ cup unsweetened instant
    tea powder
1 teaspoon cinnamon
½ teaspoon cloves
½ teaspoon nutmeg

Mix together drink mix, dry lemonade, sugar, tea powder, and spices.

Yield: 20 cups of tea.

As a Gift: Present this Vitamin C–packed tea mix in a decorated
Christmas tin with lid that seals well. Include on your greeting tag
a serving suggestion: *2 heaping teaspoons per cup of boiling water.*
Great drink to sip when you have a cold!

Hot Cocoa Mix

5 cups instant dry milk powder
2½ cups powdered sugar
1 cup unsweetened cocoa powder

1 cup powdered non-dairy creamer
1 teaspoon salt

In large mixing bowl, combine milk powder, powdered sugar, cocoa powder, salt, and creamer. Stir till thoroughly combined. Store cocoa mixture in an airtight container. For 1 serving, place ⅓ cup cocoa mixture in coffee cup or mug and add ¾ cup boiling water. Stir to dissolve. Top with dollop of whipped cream or a few marshmallows, if desired. Tip: You can vary the flavor of the cocoa by using flavored non-dairy creamers. *Yield: about 20 cups.*

As a Gift: Present your gift in a pretty antique canning jar with a snap-down ring seal. Tie a bow around the neck of the jar and paste your greeting and directions for mixing right to the jar.

Mulled Cider Mix

2 cups sweetened instant cider mix
1 teaspoon cinnamon

½ teaspoon ground cloves
¼ teaspoon salt

Mix together cider mix, spices, and salt.

Yield: about 16 cups.

As a Gift: Present your cider in a decorative tin or pretty glass jar. Make a greeting tag and tie it to the neck of the container with raffia. Include a serving suggestion: *Add 2 tablespoons mix to a cup of boiling water.*

Marshmallow Stars

1 bag large marshmallows

Roll marshmallows flat with rolling pin. Using miniature cookie cutter, cut flat stars out of each marshmallow. Place flattened stars on a waxed paper–covered cookie sheet. Cover stars with another sheet of waxed paper and place another weighted cookie sheet on top to keep stars flat as they dry out. Allow several days for drying.

Yield: 30 to 40 stars.

As a Gift: These marshmallow stars are fun to give along with a hot cocoa mix gift. Bag them in clear culinary or gift bags tied at the top with ribbon and attach them to the neck of the hot cocoa mix.

Chocolate Haystacks

2 cups semisweet chocolate chips
1 (12 ounce) can sweetened
    condensed milk
2 cups pretzel sticks, broken in
    ½-inch pieces

1 cup dry roasted peanuts
½ cup miniature candy-coated
    chocolate bits

Melt chocolate chips and milk in heavy saucepan over low heat. Stir constantly until melted and smooth. Do not boil. Remove from heat and let rest 5 minutes. In large bowl, toss pretzel sticks, peanuts, and chocolate bits until evenly combined. Gently fold in melted chocolate mixture. Working quickly, drop mixture by teaspoonfuls onto baking sheets lined with waxed paper. Refrigerate at least two hours.

Yield: about 2 dozen candies.

As a Gift: Place each candy in a paper cup wrapper and arrange on a pretty hostess plate you are gifting. Bundle all in cellophane wrap and tie with a bow.

Peanut Butter Bark

2 cups milk chocolate chips,
    divided
2 cups peanut butter chips

½ teaspoon salt
1 cup dry roasted peanuts

Line cookie sheet with waxed paper. Melt 1¾ cups milk chocolate chips, all peanut butter chips, and salt in a large saucepan over low heat, stirring frequently until smooth. Or melt the chips in a large bowl in the microwave on medium for 2 to 4 minutes, stirring once during cooking. Remove from heat and stir in remaining ¼ cup of chocolate chips until mixture is smooth. Stir in peanuts. Spread mixture on cookie sheet lined with waxed paper and refrigerate about 1 hour. Break into pieces and store in tightly covered container.

Yield: about 2½ dozen pieces.

As a Gift: Present your gift in a pretty candy bowl you are gifting. Choose a brightly decorated cellophane Christmas wrap and bundle the bowl at the top with a ribbon.

Christmas Caramels

5 cups sugar
1 pint light cream
1 quart milk
2 cups light corn syrup

½ teaspoon salt
½ teaspoon almond extract
1 teaspoon vanilla
1 cup nuts, optional

Cook sugar, cream, milk, corn syrup, and salt to hardball stage (248 degrees on candy thermometer). Add extracts and nuts. Pour into greased jelly roll pan. Cut and wrap in waxed paper cubes when cool.

Yield: about 2 dozen caramels.

As a Gift: Place wrapped caramels in a tissue-lined box or Christmas tin for presentation. Add a handwritten Christmas greeting.

Divinity Fudge

4 cups sugar
1 cup light corn syrup
½ cup water
¼ teaspoon salt

2 egg whites, beaten until frothy
1 cup chopped nuts, optional
1 teaspoon vanilla

Boil sugar, corn syrup, water, and salt to soft ball stage (forms a ball in cold water). Slowly add hot syrup to egg whites. Beat until mixture looks like fudge, then add nuts and vanilla. Spread into 9x13-inch greased pan. Cool. *Yield: about 2 dozen cubes.*

As a Gift: Cut fudge into cubes and wrap in Christmas-colored foil. Present it in a pretty jar tied with ribbon at the neck.

Holiday Chocolate Fudge

3 cups sugar
1½ sticks butter
⅔ cup evaporated milk
1 (12 ounce) package chocolate
   chips

1 (7 ounce) jar marshmallow cream
½ teaspoon salt
½ teaspoon vanilla
1 cup chopped walnuts, optional

Bring sugar, butter, and milk to full boil, stirring constantly, to soft ball stage (forms a soft ball in cold water). Remove from heat and stir in chocolate chips until melted. Add marshmallow cream, salt, vanilla, and nuts. Spread into 9x13-inch pan and cut into cubes when cool.

Yield: 3 pounds.

As a Gift: Present fudge cubes wrapped in foil and placed in a sleigh gift holder so the cubes look like wrapped gifts. (These gift containers come in all shapes and sizes at your local craft store.) Attach a bow or bundle it all up in clear plastic wrap. This recipe is ideal for 2 or even 3 gifts.

Special Treat Granola

2 cups whole oats
1 cup shredded coconut
½ cup wheat germ
½ cup walnuts, chopped
½ cup almonds, sliced or whole
1 teaspoon salt

1 (14 ounce) can sweetened
　condensed milk
¼ cup oil
¾ cup raisins
½ cup dates, chopped

Combine oats, coconut, wheat germ, nuts, and salt in large bowl.
Stir in condensed milk. Add oil and mix well. Spread on cookie sheet
lined with waxed paper and bake at 300 degrees for about an hour,
stirring occasionally. Remove from oven and cool slightly.
Stir in raisins and dates.
Yield: 8 cups.

As a Gift: Present this gift to the health-conscious friend on your
Christmas list. Buy a pretty jar or tin with a tight-fitting lid.
Top it off with a Christmas bow.

Christmas Mints

1 (8 ounce) package cream cheese
   (room temperature)
¼ to ½ teaspoon flavoring
   (peppermint, butter, almond,
   wintergreen, other)

Food coloring
Up to 3 cups powdered sugar
Sugar, as needed

Allow cream cheese to soften. Add flavoring and coloring. Gradually add powdered sugar. Mix and knead until reaching consistency of pie dough or putty. Roll into marble-sized balls. Dip in sugar and press firmly into candy mold. Unmold at once onto waxed paper. Once firm, transfer onto cake rack and let dry for 2 hours. Store in an air-tight container.

Yield: about 6 dozen.

As a Gift: Present these pretty mints in a candy dish you are gifting. Bundle all in cellophane wrap and tie with a velvet bow.

Peanut Brittle

1 cup sugar
½ cup light corn syrup

1 cup salted peanuts
1 teaspoon baking soda

Bring sugar and corn syrup to rolling boil. Stir in peanuts and keep boiling until mixture turns light tan. Remove from heat and add soda. Stir well and pour onto well-buttered cookie sheet.

Cool and break into pieces.

Yield: about 1 pound.

As a Gift: Arrange peanut brittle in a waxed paper–lined gift tin or candy jar. Write out an encouraging scripture or one related to Christmas on a small note card. Punch a hole in one end and push a ribbon through. Tie around the top of the jar and make a bow.

Peanut Butter Kisses

1 cup dark corn syrup
1 cup peanut butter
1½ cups nonfat dry milk

1 cup powdered sugar
3 cups crisp rice cereal

Mix corn syrup and peanut butter together well. Add dry milk and sugar.
Stir until mixture is smooth. Add cereal. Roll into marble-sized balls.
Let set on waxed paper until firm.

Yield: 2 dozen kisses.

As a Gift: Twist each ball into pretty candy wrappers and scatter them
in a gift basket with a new set of Christmassy kitchen towels.

Peppermint Cocoa Mix

16 ounces non-dairy creamer
8 cups nonfat dry milk
1 pound powdered sugar

3 tablespoons dark cocoa
Dash salt
1 cup crushed candy cane

Mix together creamer, milk, sugar, cocoa, salt, and crushed
candy canes. Store in lidded container.

Yield: about 12 cups of mix.

As a Gift: Present your gift in a lidded bright Christmas tin. Tie a ribbon
to the top of the tin and attach a label and greeting. Tie a bundle of tiny
candy canes into the ribbon. Include a serving suggestion: *Use ⅓ cup cocoa
mix per cup of hot water.*

Delicious Date Balls

16 ounces dates, pitted and
   chopped
2 cups sugar
2 beaten eggs
½ cup butter

¼ teaspoon salt
1 teaspoon vanilla
3½ cups crisp rice cereal
1 cup nuts, chopped
Coconut

Combine dates, sugar, eggs, butter, and salt. Cook over low heat until
smooth. Don't boil. Remove from heat and add vanilla. In large bowl,
mix cereal and nuts. Pour hot mixture over cereal mixture and stir well.
With buttered hands, form mixture into balls. Roll in coconut.

Yield: 4 dozen balls.

As a Gift: Present these pretty candies on a
pedestal plate lined with a doily. Stretch plastic
wrap over the candy and top with a bow.

Holiday Popcorn Balls

1½ cups light corn syrup
1 cup sugar
½ cup cream

½ teaspoon salt
6 to 8 cups popped corn

Mix together corn syrup, sugar, cream, and salt in heavy saucepan.
Cook to soft ball stage. Pour over popcorn, and with
buttered hands, form into balls.

Yield: about 1 dozen popcorn balls.

As a Gift: This is a great gift for the kids on your Christmas list! Wrap
each ball individually in colored kitchen wrap and present them nestled
in a tissue-lined Christmas gift bag. Tie simple Christmas tree ornaments
clustered together with a ribbon at the bag
handle—one for each member of the family.

Chocolate-Covered Strawberries

2 cups semisweet chocolate chips

12 large, ripe, long-stemmed
strawberries

4 ounces white melting chocolate

Melt semisweet chocolate according to package instructions. Holding the stem, dip berries into melted chocolate up to the shoulder (some of the bright red of the berry should be visible). Place berries on their sides on waxed paper to set. As dark chocolate firms, melt white chocolate and drizzle in stripes across resting berries.

Yield: 1 dozen strawberries.

As a Gift: This gets the blue ribbon for decadent desserts! These treats look hard to make, but they are so easy! Your recipient will be honored that you went to so much trouble! Present the berries on a doily-covered dish bundled into cellophane wrap and tied with a festive ribbon.

Chocolate-Covered Cherries

1 (8 ounce) package milk chocolate   24 large dried sweet cherries
  melting chocolate

Melt chocolate according to package directions. Using a toothpick, dip
each cherry into chocolate until well coated and place on waxed paper.
Using another toothpick for leverage, pull dipping pick
out of cherry and allow to set.

Yield: 2 dozen.

As a Gift: Fill a pretty clear Christmas jar with these delectable candies.
Be sure it has a tight-fitting lid. Use a bright red fabric ribbon tied to the
top of the jar. Label the jar with your greeting.

Caramel Apples

5 or 6 granny smith apples   2 bags wrapped caramels

Wash and dry apples. Remove stems and push popsicle stick deep into stem hole. Unwrap caramels and melt on low heat in heavy saucepan. Stir constantly and do not allow mixture to scorch. When smooth, dip apples within couple inches of stick. Let excess drip off and place on waxed paper to cool and set. (Variations include: rolling dipped apples in chopped peanuts, crushed pretzels, or crushed candy canes.)

Yield: 5 to 6 apples.

As a Gift: Wrap each apple individually in cellophane wrap and tie with curling ribbon. Present apples one at a time (on coworkers' desks, for example), or together in a lined Christmas basket for a family.

Rock Candy

2 cups sugar	½ teaspoon flavored oil
½ cup corn syrup	Food coloring
½ cup water	1 cup powdered sugar

Using candy thermometer, cook sugar, corn syrup, and water to hard crack stage, 300 degrees. Remove from heat and add oil and food coloring. Pour quickly onto greased cookie sheet. Cool and then press a hard object into candy to fracture it into small pieces. Place cool candy in bag with powdered sugar. Shake to coat very lightly. Place candy in colander and shake again to remove all but light dusting of sugar.

Yield: about 1½ pounds.

As a Gift: This beautiful candy gives the appearance of stained glass and presents beautifully in a clear glass candy dish you are gifting. Tip: make several batches, each with a different flavoring and color. Mix the colors for presentation.

Cookies
and Bars

If we think of our heart, rather than our purse, as the
reservoir of our giving, we shall find it full all the time!

DAVID DUNN

Christmas M&M Cookies

1 cup shortening
½ cup sugar
1 cup packed brown sugar
2 eggs
2 teaspoons vanilla

2¼ cups flour
1 teaspoon baking soda
¾ teaspoon salt
2 cups Christmas M&Ms

Cream together shortening, sugars, eggs, and vanilla. Combine flour, baking soda, and salt. Stir into shortening mixture. Add M&Ms. Mix and bake at 350 degrees for 10 to 12 minutes.

Yield: 3 dozen.

As a Gift: Present cookies in a parchment-lined sewing basket you are gifting. Nestle cookies in colorful tissue paper and top with another sheet of parchment to keep from staining the basket lid.

Mrs. Santa's Cinnamon Cookies

½ cup butter
½ cup shortening
1 egg yolk
1 tablespoon light corn syrup

2 cups flour
1¼ teaspoons baking soda
1 tablespoon cinnamon

Cream together butter, shortening, egg yolk, and corn syrup. Combine flour, baking soda, and cinnamon. Mix with butter mixture and chill 1 hour. Form into balls and place on ungreased cookie sheet. Press with a fork dipped in sugar. Bake at 375 degrees for 10 to 12 minutes. Let cookies set for 5 minutes.

Yield: 2 dozen cookies.

As a Gift: Present your cookies on a doily-lined sturdy plastic plate. Bundle all with cellophane wrap and tie with a bow.

Pecan Care Bears

1 cup butter
¼ cup sugar
2 teaspoons vanilla

2 cups flour
½ teaspoon salt
2½ cups pecans

Cream together butter, sugar, and vanilla. Combine flour, salt, and pecans.
Mix well. Form dough into 2-inch balls. Bake on ungreased
cookie sheet at 325 degrees for about 15 minutes.
Cool slightly and roll in powdered sugar.
Yield: 3 dozen cookies.

As a Gift: Arrange these pretty cookies gently in a tall, clear glass jar with
a tight-fitting lid. Tie a ribbon at the neck. Use a sticky label attached to
the jar to present your greeting.

Peanut Butter Cup Cookies

1 cup butter, softened	3½ cups flour
1 cup peanut butter	2 teaspoons baking soda
1 cup sugar	1 teaspoon salt
1 cup packed brown sugar	1 (16 ounce) package miniature
2 eggs	peanut butter cups
2 teaspoons vanilla	

Blend butter, peanut butter, and sugars until creamy. Add eggs and vanilla. Mix well. Combine flour, baking soda, and salt. Add to creamed mixture. Shape dough into balls that fit nicely into ungreased miniature muffin tins. Bake at 350 degrees for 5 to 7 minutes. Don't overbake. Remove from oven and press one mini peanut butter cup into center of each cookie. Let cool in muffin tin.

Yield: 3 dozen cookies.

As a Gift: These cookies are small and fit easily in candy cup wrappers, available in cooking and craft stores. Place cupped cookies close together in a shallow, lidded Christmas box. Top with a bow and your greeting.

French Lace

1 cup flour
1 cup walnuts, finely chopped
½ cup light corn syrup

½ cup shortening
⅔ cup packed brown sugar

Blend flour and walnuts. Bring corn syrup, shortening, and sugar to boil over medium heat, stirring constantly. Remove from heat and gradually add flour mixture. Drop batter by teaspoonfuls onto lightly greased cookie sheet. Bake just a few cookies at a time at 375 degrees for 5 to 6 minutes. Allow to cool for 5 minutes before removing from baking sheet.

Yield: 1 dozen cookies.

. . . .

As a Gift: These delicate, lacy cookies will look pretty in a short stack of 4 or 5, wrapped in Christmas kitchen wrap and topped with a bow.

Christmas Tea Cookies

½ cup shortening
¼ cup butter
½ cup powdered sugar
1½ cups flour

¼ teaspoon salt
2 eggs
1 teaspoon vanilla
¼ cup chopped nuts, optional

Cream together shortening, butter, and sugar. Combine flour and salt and gently blend into creamed mixture. Don't overwork. Add beaten eggs and vanilla. Add nuts. Chill dough for 2 hours, shape into balls, and roll in powdered sugar. Place on cookie sheet and flatten gently. Bake at 350 degrees for 20 minutes.

Yield: 2 dozen cookies.

As a Gift: Present these cookies in a small, clear bag tied with ribbon, 2 or 3 cookies to the bag. Place the bag in a tea cup with saucer you are gifting. Insert a couple of wrapped tea bags in with the cookies. Bundle it all in cellophane wrap and tie with a ribbon.

Peppermint Meringue Drops

4 egg whites
¼ teaspoon salt
¼ teaspoon cream of tartar

1 teaspoon peppermint extract
1½ cups sugar

In mixing bowl, beat egg whites, salt, cream of tartar, and extract until soft peaks form. Add sugar gradually until mixture forms stiff peaks. Drop by teaspoonfuls onto parchment-covered cookie sheet. Bake at 300 degrees for 20 minutes or until very lightly browned. Let meringues harden before removing from sheet.

Yield: 1½ dozen cookies.

As a gift: Bag meringue drops in a clear plastic bag and tie with ribbon. Place it in a small tissue- or cloth-lined basket along with some really good pure chocolate bars. The drops and chocolate are a great combination, so attach a label with that suggestion and your greeting.

Old-Fashioned Molasses Cookies

3 cups flour
2 teaspoons baking soda
1 teaspoon salt
1 teaspoon ginger
1 teaspoon cinnamon
¾ cup evaporated milk

¾ tablespoon cider vinegar
1 cup shortening
1 cup sugar
1 egg
½ cup molasses

Stir together flour, baking soda, salt, and spices. Combine evaporated milk and vinegar. Cream shortening and sugar thoroughly. Add egg and molasses. Beat well. Add milk and vinegar mixture alternately with dry mixture. Mix well. Drop by teaspoonfuls onto greased cookie sheet. Bake at 375 degrees for 10 minutes. Do not overbake.

Yield: 4 dozen cookies.

As a Gift: Line cookies on end like dominoes in shallow, cardboard gift box. These come plain or decorated in cooking and hobby stores. Bundle all in cellophane wrap and tie the top with a bow.

Orange Iced Cranberry Cookies

½ cup butter, softened
¾ cup sugar
½ cup packed brown sugar
½ cup sour cream
1 teaspoon vanilla
2 eggs
2¼ cups flour

½ teaspoon baking soda
½ teaspoon baking powder
½ teaspoon salt
1 cup fresh cranberries or Craisins, chopped
1 can buttercream frosting

In large bowl, cream together butter, sugars, sour cream, vanilla, and eggs. Add flour, baking soda, baking powder, and salt. Mix well. Stir in cranberries gently. Drop by teaspoonfuls onto lightly greased baking sheet and bake at 350 degrees for 12 minutes. Cool and frost with frosting.
Yield: 2½ dozen cookies.

As a gift: Buy some really beautiful navel oranges and arrange them among the cookies in a bread basket you're gifting. Oranges are really good this time of year, and always welcome!

7-Layer Christmas Bars

1 stick butter
1 cup graham cracker crumbs
1 cup shredded coconut
1 cup pecans, chopped
1 cup milk chocolate chips

1 cup butterscotch chips
1 cup semisweet chocolate chips
1 (12 ounce) can sweetened
   condensed milk

Melt butter in 8x8-inch baking pan. Stir in graham cracker crumbs and pat evenly in bottom. Sprinkle coconut, pecans, and chips over crumbs in layers. Pour milk evenly over top. Bake at 350 degrees for 25 to 30 minutes. Let cool and cut into bars.

Yield: 9 to 12 bars.

As a Gift: Present bars on a stack of pretty dessert plates you are gifting. Bundle it all in cellophane wrap and tie with a ribbon.

Lemon Bars

½ cup butter or margarine
1 cup flour
¼ cup powdered sugar
2 eggs
2 tablespoons flour
1 cup sugar

3 tablespoons lemon juice
½ teaspoon salt
½ teaspoon baking powder
Powdered sugar, as needed
  for dusting

Blend butter, flour, and sugar. Press into 8x11-inch pan. Bake at 350 degrees for 15 minutes. Combine eggs, flour, sugar, lemon juice, salt, and baking powder. Mix well and pour over crust. Bake at 350 degrees for 20 to 25 minutes. Sprinkle powdered sugar on top. Cut into squares while still warm.

Yield: 9 to 12 bars.

As a Gift: Present these bars on a doily-covered plate. Arrange them like the numerals on a clock and put a beautiful, ripe lemon in the center. Bundle in cellophane wrap and tie the top with a bow.

Andes Mountain Squares

1¼ cups butter, divided
½ cup cocoa
3½ cups powdered sugar, divided
1 teaspoon vanilla

2 cups graham cracker crumbs
⅓ cup crème de menthe
1½ cups semisweet chocolate chips

In heavy saucepan combine ½ cup butter with cocoa. Heat and whisk until well blended. Remove from heat and add ½ cup powdered sugar. Stir in vanilla and cracker crumbs. Press into greased 9x13-inch baking pan. Melt ½ cup butter and combine with crème de menthe. Slowly beat in 3 cups powdered sugar. Spread over bottom layer. Chill 1 hour. Combine ¼ cup butter and chocolate chips. Stir over low heat until melted. Spread over mint layer. Chill 2 hours. Remove from refrigerator 15 minutes prior to serving.

Yield: 12 to 16 squares.

As a Gift: Arrange in a tissue and waxed paper–lined shallow box, like fine chocolates. Present them to a climbing enthusiast in your life!

Angel Bars

1 cup flour
4 tablespoons powdered sugar
½ cup butter, melted
1 cup sugar
1 teaspoon baking powder
¼ teaspoon salt

3 beaten eggs
3 tablespoons lemon juice
1 tablespoon lemon zest
¾ cup flaked coconut
Powdered sugar, if needed
   for dusting

Combine flour, powdered sugar, and butter. Press into 9x9-inch square baking dish. Bake at 350 degrees for 15 minutes. Combine sugar, baking powder, salt, eggs, lemon juice, lemon zest, and coconut. Mix well. Pour over slightly cooled crust. Bake at 350 degrees for 20 minutes. Sprinkle with powdered sugar when cool and cut into bars.

Yield: 12 bars.

As a Gift: Present your bars on a clear plastic plate. Bundle all in cellophane wrap and tie an angel Christmas tree ornament into the ribbon.

Cranberry Paradise Bars

2½ cups flour
2½ teaspoons baking powder
½ teaspoon salt
¼ cup butter, softened
½ cup shortening
1¾ cups packed brown sugar

3 large eggs
1 teaspoon vanilla
½ teaspoon orange flavoring
½ cup white chocolate chips
½ cup orange-flavored Craisins

Sift together flour, baking powder, and salt and set aside. Beat butter, shortening, and brown sugar until creamy. Beat in eggs, vanilla, and orange flavoring. Add flour mixture ½ cup at a time, mixing well. Stir in white chocolate chips and Craisins. Spread onto greased jelly roll pan and bake at 350 degrees for 20 minutes or until golden brown. Cool well and cut into bars.

Yield: 12 bars.

As a Gift: Present these pretty and incredibly yummy bars on a doily-lined Christmas plate you're gifting. Bundle with cellophane wrap and tie with a bow.

Chocolate Pizza

1 cup shortening
1 cup packed brown sugar
½ cup sugar
2 eggs
1 teaspoon vanilla

2¼ cups flour
1 teaspoon baking soda
½ teaspoon salt
Assorted candy bars, roughly
    chopped into chunks

Cream together shortening, sugars, eggs, and vanilla. Combine flour, baking soda, and salt. Stir into creamed mixture. Press cookie dough into greased 9x9-inch baking pan and bake at 350 degrees for 15 to 20 minutes. Remove from oven and spread thick layer of chopped candy bars over. Return to oven for 5 minutes. Turn off oven but leave pan in for 10 minutes or until candy bars are melted but still slightly chunky. Remove from oven. When nearly cool, and before candy hardens again, cut into bars.

Yield: 10 slices.

As a Gift: A very fun gift! Present it whole on a new pizza stone you're gifting.

Apricot Balls

1 (8 ounce) package dried apricots, finely diced
2½ cups flaked coconut

¾ cup sweetened condensed milk
1 cup nuts, finely chopped (pecans work especially well)

Mix together apricots, coconut, and milk. Shape into 1-inch balls and roll in nuts. Refrigerate.

Yield: 1½ dozen.

As a Gift: These rich, festive cookies will look pretty presented in a candy dish or interesting serving bowl you are gifting. Bundle in cellophane wrap and tie a bow at the top.

Christmas Hands

1 cup shortening
2 cups sugar
2 eggs
½ cup milk
5 cups flour
1 teaspoon baking soda

1 teaspoon baking powder
½ teaspoon salt
1 teaspoon lemon flavoring
1 (16 ounce) can buttercream frosting
Assorted sprinkles and candies for
  decorating

Cream together shortening and sugar. Add eggs and milk. Mix well. Combine flour, baking soda, baking powder, salt, and lemon flavoring. Blend into creamed mixture. Roll ¼ of dough at a time, as gently as possible, to about ¼ inch. Cut around your children's hand shapes. Bake on greased cookie sheet at 350 degrees for 8 to 10 minutes. Cool. Frost with buttercream frosting and decorate. *Yield: 4 dozen cookies.*

As a Gift: A very fun and unique treat for grandparents, teachers, aunts, uncles, and cousins! Let your kids decorate them with their names included. Wrap each hand individually in a plastic bag and tie the top with a ribbon.

Gingerbread Men

1 cup packed brown sugar
⅓ cup shortening
1½ cups dark molasses
⅔ cup water
7 cups flour
2 teaspoons baking soda
1 teaspoon salt

2 teaspoons ginger
1 teaspoon allspice
1 teaspoon cloves
1 teaspoon cinnamon
1 (16 ounce) can frosting
   (any flavor)

Cream together sugar and shortening. Add molasses and water. Mix well. Stir in flour, baking soda, salt, and spices. Cover and refrigerate 2 hours. Roll out ¼ of dough at a time to ½-inch thickness. Cut with gingerbread man cookie cutter and place cookies on lightly greased cookie sheet. Leave plenty of room between each cookie. Bake at 350 degrees for 10 to 12 minutes. Cool, frost, and decorate. *Yield: 3 dozen cookies.*

As a Gift: Wrap each gingerbread man in a clear kitchen bag and tie the top with a ribbon. Give each cookie a nametag to make it as individual as the child receiving it.

Candy Cane Cookies

1 cup shortening
1 cup powdered sugar
1 egg
1½ teaspoons almond flavoring
1 teaspoon vanilla
2½ cups flour

1 teaspoon salt
¼ teaspoon baking soda
Red food coloring
6 large candy canes, crushed
Sugar, as needed

Mix shortening, sugar, egg, almond flavoring, and vanilla thoroughly.
Add flour, salt, and baking soda. Divide dough in half and blend
red food coloring into one half. Roll out each half separately and cut into
4-inch strips. For each cookie, twist strips together (candy-cane style)
and shape like a candy cane. Bake at 350 degrees for 10 minutes.
While still hot, sprinkle with mixture of crushed
peppermint candy canes and sugar.

Yield: about 6 cookies.

As a Gift: Arrange 2 to 4 candy cane cookies in a
tissue-lined, shallow clear plastic box (available in
craft and food stores).

Old-Fashioned Gingersnaps

2 cups dark molasses
½ cup packed brown sugar
½ cup water
1 cup shortening

2 teaspoons ground ginger
6½ cups flour
2 teaspoons baking soda
½ teaspoon salt

Cook molasses, sugar, and water in saucepan on low heat for 15 minutes.
Remove from heat and add shortening and ginger. Set aside until cool.
Add flour, baking soda, and salt. Mix well. Dough should be very stiff.
Refrigerate for 2 hours. Roll out as thin as possible on floured board.
Cut into small circles and bake on greased cookie sheet at
375 degrees about 6 to 8 minutes or until slightly brown.

Yield: 7 dozen snaps.

As a Gift: These classic Christmas cookies will present well in a clear
cellophane bag with a tent label stapled to the top. Include
your greeting on the tent and hole punch for a ribbon to tie into.

Rosemary Crescents

½ cup shortening
1 cup sugar
1 egg
5 cups flour
1 teaspoon baking powder

1 teaspoon baking soda
½ teaspoon salt
1 teaspoon dried rosemary,
    finely ground
1 cup buttermilk

Cream together shortening, sugar, and egg. Combine flour, baking powder, baking soda, salt, and rosemary. Add to creamed mixture alternately with buttermilk. Chill dough for 2 hours. Roll out to ½-inch thickness on floured board and cut into circles with cookie cutter. Halve each cookie and gently shape into crescent. Bake on greased cookie sheet at 350 degrees for 10 minutes. While cookies are still warm, dust very lightly with powdered sugar.

Yield: 6 dozen crescents.

As a gift: Nestle these unusual tea cookies into a gift tin lined with waxed paper. Tie up the tin with ribbon and insert a few sprigs of fresh rosemary into the bow.

Shortbread

1 cup shortening	2 teaspoons vanilla
½ cup sugar	2¾ cups flour
½ cup packed brown sugar	2 teaspoons cream of tartar
3 egg yolks	1 teaspoon baking soda
¼ cup milk	½ teaspoon salt

Cream together shortening, sugars, and egg yolks. Add milk and vanilla. Combine flour, cream of tartar, baking soda, and salt. Stir into creamed mixture. Chill 1 hour. Roll out to ½-inch thickness on floured board. Cut into long strips and then cut again across strips to form 2-inch squares. Bake on ungreased cookie sheet at 350 degrees for 10 to 12 minutes.

Yield: 3 dozen shortbread squares.

As a Gift: Arrange the shortbread in waxed paper in a square Scottish-looking tin. Include a packet of fine tea or a small tea brewing ball as a gift.

Grapefruit Sugar Cookies

½ cup shortening
½ cup butter
1 cup sugar
2 eggs
2½ cups flour

2 teaspoons baking powder
½ teaspoon salt
¾ cup candied grapefruit peel,
    finely chopped

Cream together shortening, butter, sugar, and eggs. Combine flour, baking powder, salt, and grapefruit peel. Add to creamed mixture. Roll dough to ¼-inch thickness on floured board. Cut into squares or circles. Bake on greased cookie sheet at 350 degrees for 10 minutes.

Yield: 3 dozen cookies.

As a Gift: Locate a nice bag of Florida, Texas, or California grapefruit and present it along with a plate of these delicious and unusual cookies.

Cinnamon Nut Cookies

1 cup shortening
1 cup sugar
4 eggs
1 teaspoon vanilla
4 cups flour
1 teaspoon baking powder

½ teaspoon salt
1 cup pecans, chopped
Cinnamon sugar
Red hots (cookie decoration
    candies)

Cream together shortening and sugar. Add eggs and vanilla. Combine flour, baking powder, and salt. Blend with creamed mixture. Add nuts. Chill in refrigerator for several hours. Form dough into 2 or 3 long rolls and bake on greased cookie sheet at 350 degrees for about 30 minutes. While rolls are still warm, slice into ½-inch slices. Place on cookie sheet and sprinkle with cinnamon sugar. Place a red hot candy décor piece in center of each cookie and bake an additional 10 minutes. *Yield: 4 dozen cookies.*

As a Gift: Arrange these spicy treats in the plastic wrap–lined well of a new nut bowl you're gifting. Bundle in clear gift wrap. Include a small bag of unshelled mixed nuts.

Jam Thumbprints

1 (8 ounce) package cream cheese
¾ cup butter, softened
1 cup powdered sugar
2¼ cups flour
½ teaspoon baking soda
½ cup pecans, chopped
½ teaspoon vanilla
Fruit jam or preserves

Beat cream cheese, butter, and powdered sugar until smooth. Add flour and baking soda. Mix well. Add pecans and vanilla. Chill dough for 30 minutes. Shape dough into 1-inch balls and place on ungreased cookie sheet. Press thumb in middle of each cookie. Fill with about 1 teaspoon of your favorite jam or fruit preserves. Bake in 350 degree oven for 14 to 16 minutes. *Yield: 3 dozen cookies.*

As a Gift: Present these delicious cookies on a plastic Christmas plate, bundle with cellophane wrap, and tie a new pair of winter gloves or mittens into the bow.

Italian Christmas Cookies

½ cup butter
½ cup shortening
1 cup sugar
5 eggs
1 teaspoon vanilla
5 cups flour
3 teaspoons baking powder
½ teaspoon salt

FILLING:
1 cup sweetened applesauce or
   apple butter
½ cup walnuts, crushed
CHOCOLATE COATING:
Sugar, as needed
1 cup semisweet chocolate chips
1 tablespoon butter

Cream together butter, shortening, and sugar. Stir in eggs and vanilla. Combine flour, baking powder, and salt. Add to creamed mixture and mix well. Chill. Roll out to ¼-inch thickness on floured board and cut into 3-inch squares. Filling: Combine applesauce and walnuts. Add 1 teaspoon of filling. Fold diagonally to form triangle. Crimp edges and sprinkle lightly with sugar. Bake at 375 degrees for about 10 minutes. Melt chocolate chips and butter. Dip half of each triangle in 3chocolate and let set on waxed paper. *Yield: 2 dozen cookies.*

As a Gift: Present these cookies to the music lover on your list. Include a CD of their favorite Italian opera.

Holiday Fruit Drops

1 cup shortening
2 cups packed brown sugar
2 eggs
½ cup sour milk
3½ cups flour
1 teaspoon baking soda

1 teaspoon salt
2 cups candied cherries,
  halved or chopped
2 cups dates, chopped
1½ cups pecan halves, divided

Cream shortening and sugar. Add eggs. Stir in sour milk. Combine flour, baking soda, and salt. Add to creamed mixture. Stir in cherries, dates, and half of pecans. Chill for 1 hour. Drop by rounded teaspoonfuls onto lightly greased cookie sheet. Place pecan half on each cookie and bake at 400 degrees for 8 to 10 minutes. (These cookies actually *improve* with storage.) *Yield: 3 dozen cookies.*

As a Gift: Present these cookies in a tin reminiscent of old fruitcake containers. Scout antique and secondhand shops for interesting container ideas! A really nice alternative to fruit*cake*!

Banana Bars

¾ cup shortening
¾ cup sugar
1 egg
1 mashed banana
1½ cups flour
½ teaspoon baking powder
¼ teaspoon baking soda

½ teaspoon salt
¾ teaspoon cinnamon
¼ teaspoon allspice
¼ cup milk
½ cup nuts, chopped
1 (16 ounce) can buttercream
    frosting

Cream together shortening and sugar. Add egg and banana. Mix well.
Combine flour, baking powder, baking soda, salt, and spices. Add to
creamed mixture alternating with milk. Add nuts. Bake in 9x13-inch
pan at 350 degrees for 20 minutes. Ice with buttercream frosting
while still slightly warm. Cool and cut into bars.

Yield: 12 to 16 bars.

As a Gift: A very rich and delicious dessert bar! Line them up
in a waxed paper–lined soft thermal lunch box you are gifting.
Tie a big bow to the handle.

Christmas Bells

1 cup butter	FROSTING:
½ cup sugar	¼ cup butter
1 egg	2 to 3 cups powdered sugar
½ teaspoon almond extract	½ teaspoon almond extract
2½ cups flour	Milk, as needed

Cream together butter and sugar. Add egg and extract. Add flour all at once and blend, but don't overmix. Chill for 1 hour. Roll out to ½-inch thickness and cut out with bell cookie cutter. Bake on lightly greased cookie sheet at 350 degrees for 10 to 12 minutes. Frosting: Combine butter, sugar, and almond extract. Blend together, adding milk one tablespoon at a time until right consistency is reached.

Yield: 2 dozen cookies.

As a Gift: Present your bell cookies stacked like crackers in a disposable Christmas food box. Tie the cutter into the ribbon as a gift.

Soup to Nuts

*A man's gift maketh room for him,
and bringeth him before great men.*

PROVERBS 18:16

Cheese Wafers

2 cups sharp cheddar cheese,
  finely grated
¼ cup butter, softened
1 cup flour

½ teaspoon salt
¼ teaspoon cayenne pepper
½ cup walnuts, finely chopped

Combine cheese and butter. Add flour, salt, and cayenne pepper. Fold in nuts. Form dough into 2 logs and refrigerate for 2 hours. Slice and bake on greased cookie sheet at 350 degrees for not more than 5 minutes or until light brown. Very delicate. Do not overbake.

Yield: 3 to 4 dozen.

As a Gift: A great Christmas appetizer! Present it on an appetizer plate along with a small roll of summer sausage.

Barley Lentil Soup in a Jar

½ cup barley
½ cup dried split peas
½ cup white basmati rice
½ cup dry lentils
2 tablespoons dried minced onion
1 tablespoon dried parsley

2 teaspoons salt
1 teaspoon pepper
2 tablespoons dry beef bouillon
½ cup uncooked pasta
Uncooked macaroni (any style)

In wide mouth, 1-quart jar, layer barley, peas, rice, and lentils.
Then layer in onion, parsley, salt, pepper, bouillon,
and pasta. Fill remainder of jar with macaroni.

As a Gift: Tie a fabric topper to the lid with raffia and include this
suggested recipe: *Add contents of jar to 3 quarts of water, 2 stalks of chopped
celery, 2 sliced carrots, and 2 cups diced tomatoes. Over medium-low heat,
cover and simmer about 25 minutes, or until vegetables are tender.*
Yield: about 3½ quarts.

Chicken Soup in a Bag

3 tablespoons dried chicken
  bouillon
½ teaspoon salt
½ teaspoon pepper

¼ teaspoon paprika
½ teaspoon celery salt
1 teaspoon dried parsley
½ cup uncooked instant rice

Combine bouillon, salt, pepper, paprika, celery salt, parsley, and rice.

As a Gift: A great gift for coworkers or neighbors! Present dry ingredients in a small clear gift bag folded several times at the top. Staple on a tented label greeting and hole punch it to create a spot for the ribbon. Include the preparation directions inside the bag, or on the label: *Add to 1 quart water in saucepan and simmer for 15 minutes. (Add any fresh vegetables you wish!) Yield: 4 cups of soup.*

Cheesy Potato Soup in a Jar

1 cup dried mashed potato flakes
¼ cup dried parmesan cheese
3 tablespoons dry chicken bouillon
1 teaspoon salt
½ teaspoon pepper

½ teaspoon paprika
½ teaspoon celery salt
1 teaspoon dried parsley flakes
Instant dry nonfat milk flakes

In 1-pint canning jar, layer potato flakes, cheese, and bouillon.
Sprinkle in seasonings and top with parsley flakes.
Fill remainder of space with dried milk.

As a Gift: Cover jar with a burlap topper tied on with ribbon. Along with your greeting, include the soup name and directions for preparation on the label: *Stir contents of jar into 2 quarts boiling water and ½ cup diced veggies: carrots, celery, peas, etc. (optional). Simmer until vegetables are tender. Yield: 2 quarts.*

133

Alphabet Soup in a Jar

½ cup dry chicken bouillon crystals ½ teaspoon dried onion
½ teaspoon paprika   Dash pepper
½ teaspoon celery salt   Alphabet macaroni
1 teaspoon dried parsley

Mix bouillon crystals, paprika, salt, parsley, onion, and pepper. Pour into
1-pint jar. Fill remainder of space with macaroni.

As a Gift: A very fun gift for a child, because you only have to add water
to make soup. Screw on the lid and decorate. Include the recipe with
your greeting: *Add 1 quart of water to contents of jar and bring to boil. Add
macaroni and fresh or canned vegetables for color and richness. Simmer until
pasta is soft. Yield: 4 servings.*

Pumpkin Butter

1 (29 ounce) can prepared pumpkin
½ cup apple juice
2 teaspoons ginger
½ teaspoon cloves

1 teaspoon nutmeg
2 teaspoons cinnamon
1½ cups sugar
1 pound butter, room temperature

Combine pumpkin, apple juice, spices, and sugar in large saucepan. Stir well. Bring mixture to boil. Reduce heat and simmer for 30 minutes or until thickened. Stir often. Set aside to cool. When completely cool, blend in softened butter. *Yield: about 3½ cups.*

As a Gift: A terrific hostess gift! Present it in a lidded crock or wide mouthed jar with fabric topper. Be sure to include instructions: *Keep refrigerated.*

Pineapple Butter

1 pound butter, room temperature
1 (6 ounce) can pineapple, crushed
½ teaspoon lemon juice

Combine butter, pineapple, and juice. Refrigerate.

Yield: about 3 cups.

As a Gift: This festive holiday spread is beautiful and unusual. Present it in a lidded crock with a fresh loaf of French bread!

Cranberry Pecan Spread

2 cups cottage cheese, creamy style
3 tablespoons sour cream
1½ tablespoons packed brown sugar
½ cup toasted pecans, chopped
½ cup dried cranberries or cherries, chopped
½ teaspoon lemon zest

Combine cottage cheese, sour cream, sugar, pecans, cranberries, and lemon zest in blender or food processor and refrigerate.

Yield: about 3 cups.

As a Gift: Present in a lidded clear glass jar. Decorate. Include these serving instructions: *Serve on crackers, muffins, or fresh-baked bread. Keep refrigerated!*

Reindeer Mix

1 cup miniature salted pretzels
1 cup Corn Chex cereal
1 cup Rice Chex cereal
1 cup salted mixed nuts

1 cup Boston Baked Beans candy
1 cup M&Ms
1 cup dried cranberries

Mix pretzels, cereal, nuts, candy, and cranberries thoroughly.
Store in airtight container.
Yield: about 8 to 10 cups.

As a Gift: Present your gift in Christmas design disposable storage ware or lidded glass jar. Decorate with a Christmas bow or fabric topper tied with raffia.

Spicy Sweet Nuts

½ stick butter
½ cup packed brown sugar
½ teaspoon ground nutmeg
1 teaspoon ground cinnamon

½ teaspoon salt
2 tablespoons water
3 cups pecan or walnut halves

Melt butter in 9x13-inch glass baking dish in microwave. Stir in sugar, spices, salt, and water. Microwave on high for 1 minute. Stir in nuts until well coated. Microwave for 4 to 5 minutes more, stirring after each minute. Spread cooked nuts out onto waxed paper to cool.

Yield: 3 cups.

As a Gift: Present your gift in a pretty glass antique jar with a fabric topping tied with ribbon or raffia. Include these instructions:
Enjoy by the handful or sprinkled over salads, pancakes, or waffles!

Cinnamon Mixed Nuts

3 cups unsalted mixed nuts
½ cup powdered sugar

2 teaspoons ground cinnamon

Combine nuts, sugar, and cinnamon in plastic bag. Shake to coat nuts
well. Spread onto cookie sheet and bake at 285 degrees
for 1 hour, stirring occasionally.

Yield: 3 cups.

As a Gift: Enclose in clear gift bags with tented labels.
Hole punch the label to run a ribbon through.

Chocolate Coffee Spoons

1 small package milk chocolate chips
12 to 15 clear plastic spoons
½ cup large grain sugar (Christmas colors look great)
½ cup crushed candy cane

Melt chocolate chips and coat spoon bowl. Shake off excess and let set. Repeat with second coat of chocolate. Sprinkle sugar and crushed candy cane over chocolate. Place on waxed paper to set.

Yield: 12 to 15 spoons.

As a Gift: A great gift for the coffee lover on your list! Bundle several together in cellophane wrap and tie with a ribbon. Include a pound of gourmet coffee beans!

Chocolate-Covered Sugar Cubes

1 cup milk chocolate chips   1 (16 ounce) box sugar cubes

Melt chocolate. Using small tongs, dip sugar cubes in warm chocolate.
Shake off excess. Let each cube drain well over mesh drainer,
so chocolate doesn't pool as it sets.
Yield: about 20 cubes.

As a Gift: Bag these up in clear gift bags and tent label them. Attach
ribbon and greeting with a serving suggestion for sweetening coffee. In
your greeting, tell the recipient *"I love you very mocha!"*

Flavored Creams

1 pint table cream

2 teaspoons flavoring extract
or spices

Mix together cream and flavoring extract or spices of your choice.
Refrigerate.
Yield: 1 pint.

As a Gift: Flavored creams are very popular additions to coffee
year round, but during the holidays, peppermint, cinnamon, and
chocolate flavors are great. Scour antique and secondhand shops
for old milk bottles (small) with lids. Tie a bow to the neck.

Annie's Fresh Salsa

1 bunch fresh cilantro
1 bunch green onions
1 or 2 jalapeño peppers,
   ribs and seeds removed

1 (28 ounce) can crushed tomatoes
1 teaspoon salt
Garlic salt, to taste
1 (28 ounce) can diced tomatoes

Rough chop cilantro, onions, and peppers in food processor. Add salt, garlic, and tomatoes. Blend to desired consistency. Keep refrigerated.
Yield: 4 cups.

. . . .

As a Gift: Make the salsa a day before gifting it. This allows the flavors to blend well. Salsa is a welcome taste change to the typically heavy, sweet offerings over the holidays. Present salsa in a pretty Mexican bowl and matching plate you're gifting. Include a bag of crispy tortilla chips to spread around the bowl for serving.

Mango Salsa

About 1 pound mangos, very ripe
1 red bell pepper, diced
1 jalapeño pepper, ribbed, seeded, and diced
3 tablespoons fresh cilantro, chopped

2 tablespoons fresh mint, chopped
1 small red onion, diced
2 tablespoons honey
1 tablespoon lime juice
¼ teaspoon ground red pepper
½ teaspoon salt

Mix together mangos, bell pepper, jalapeño pepper, cilantro, mint, onion, honey, lime juice, red pepper, and salt. Chill.

Yield: 2 cups.

As a Gift: Present your homemade salsa in a pretty Mexican pottery bowl you are gifting. Try to find one that has a plastic lid for storage. If not, cover tightly with food wrap and give it with a bow and your greeting attached. (Include a bag of tortilla chips!)

Herbal Tea Sachets

Good loose Chai or other herbal tea, in bulk

Cheesecloth circles

Place tablespoonfuls of dry tea in cheesecloth circles and tie them up to form little teabags. Use string that won't bleed color or melt into hot water when used. *Yield: As many as you like.*

As a Gift: Tie a simple label and greeting to the end of the string. If you use a variety of teas in a single gift, be sure to package each variety in a separate clear bag so flavors don't intermingle. Place several bags together in a tea mug, teacup, or teapot you are gifting and bundle all in cellophane wrap with a bow.

Squash Soup

1 squash, halved and seeded
¼ cup butter
Salt and pepper to taste
1 quart cream

1 cup milk
1 cup chicken broth
1 teaspoon seasoned salt

Place squash halves, cut side up, in baking dish. Fill seed cup with butter. Salt and pepper. Cover with foil and bake at 350 degrees for 60 to 90 minutes. When slightly cool, scoop out all flesh from rind. Place in blender or manually mash until large clumps are worked out. Add squash, cream, milk, broth, and salt in large saucepan. Stir while it heats. Enjoy with crispy croutons and crumbled bacon as a garnish! *Yield: about 8 bowls of soup.*

As a Gift: For the veggie or soup lover on your list! Buy one of the beautiful squashes that work especially well for soup, such as butternut, acorn, etc. Wash it and rub it with a tiny bit of olive oil until it shines. Then attach a ribbon and include a recipe card explaining how to make it into soup. A very fun and original gift—economical and healthy, as well!

Curried Pecans

2 cups small pecan halves
2 teaspoons ground curry

3 teaspoons vegetable oil
Dash salt

Mix together pecans, curry, oil, and salt. Spread out on a cookie sheet and bake at 300 degrees for 30 minutes, stirring a couple times during baking. *Yield: 2 cups.*

. . . .

As a Gift: Fill a personalized new coffee mug with pecans. Bundle all in tissue paper and tie with a ribbon. Attach your greeting and label.

Chili Peanuts

½ stick butter
2½ cups raw Spanish peanuts
½ teaspoon garlic salt

½ teaspoon seasoned salt
1½ tablespoons chili powder

Melt butter and stir in peanuts, salt, and chili powder. Mix well.
Spread on a cookie sheet and bake at 300 degrees for
30 minutes, stirring every 10 minutes.

Yield: 2½ cups.

As a Gift: Fill a pretty, clear jar (these come in all shapes and sizes at
craft and dollar stores. Be sure it has a good lid) with nuts.
Label the jar and include the ingredients listed
above. Tie a ribbon around the neck of the jar for
presentation and attach your greeting.

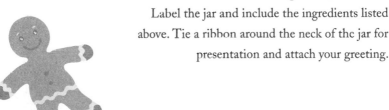

Peggy's Party Pecans

1 pound pecan halves
1 egg white
1 teaspoon water
1 cup sugar

1 teaspoon cinnamon
1 teaspoon salt
Dash salt

Wash pecan halves and gently pat dry. In large bowl, whip egg white and water to froth. Add pecans and coat well. In separate bowl, combine sugar, cinnamon, and salt. Mix well. Add to pecans, using fingers to make sure all are coated. Shake off excess sugar and spread on foil-lined cookie sheet. Bake at 225 degrees for 60 to 90 minutes, stirring every 15 minutes. Pecans will become crispy as they cool.

Yield: 1 pound.

As a Gift: Present 1 cup of pecans in a freezer bag or cello gift bag with a ribbon tie at the top. Tuck it into a cute Christmas stocking for gifting.

Spicy Snack Mix

16 ounces butter
1½ tablespoons garlic salt
1 teaspoon onion salt
4 tablespoons Worcestershire sauce
1 (12 ounce) box toasted oats cereal

1 (12 ounce) box wheat squares
  cereal
1 (10 ounce) can shoestring potatoes
1 (16 ounce) bag pretzel sticks
16 ounces salted nuts

Melt butter in large bowl. Add salt and Worcestershire sauce.
Toss together with cereal, potatoes, pretzel sticks, and nuts
until everything is well mixed. Spread on cookie
sheet and bake at 300 degrees for 30 minutes.

Yield: about 10 quarts.

As a Gift: Present the mix in a tin or plastic storage container
you are gifting. Top it with a bow. This is a welcome gift
any time of year, but especially at Christmas!

Chocolate Pots of Cream

1½ cups half-and-half
6 tablespoons sugar
½ cup semisweet chocolate chips

4 egg yolks
1 teaspoon vanilla

Place 4 small ramekins or custard dishes in square baking dish. Preheat oven to 350 degrees. Heat half-and-half and sugar until steaming. Don't let boil. Remove from heat and stir in chocolate chips until melted, stirring occasionally. Blend in egg yolks and vanilla and pour into ramekins. Boil water and fill baking dish until water is halfway up sides of ramekins. Bake in 350 degree oven for 20 minutes or until mixture is set, but still jiggly in center. Cool.
Yield: 4 servings.

As a Gift: Cover each ramekin with plastic wrap. Present them in a small box or basket lined with Christmas fabric or placed on small doilies. The ramekins are the gift.

Crème Brûlée

2 cups whipping cream
4 eggs, beaten well
2 tablespoons sugar

Dash salt
1 teaspoon vanilla
Fine brown sugar, as needed

Mix together whipping cream, eggs, sugar, salt, and vanilla. Pour into ramekins you are planning to gift. Leave room for a thin crust at top. Cover hot mixture with food wrap and cool well overnight in refrigerator. Top cold custards with light layer of fine brown sugar. Place on cookie sheet and broil until sugar turns liquid. This happens quickly. Remove and cool. Keep in refrigerator until time to present.

Yield: 3 large or 6 small servings.

As a Gift: Make the brûlée the night before gifting and do the caramelization only a few hours before you wrap it. Bundle individual ramekins of cold brûlées in cellophane wrap and tie with a bow with the instruction: *Keep refrigerated until ready to serve.*

Orange Custard Cups

2 cups whipping cream
4 eggs, beaten well
2 tablespoons sugar

Dash salt
1 teaspoon vanilla

In heavy saucepan, slowly heat cream, eggs, sugar, salt, and vanilla, stirring until the mixture is almost to boiling point. Do not boil. Cook just under boiling for 1 minute. As mixture cools slightly, arrange well-drained mandarin orange segments in bottoms of ramekins you are planning to gift. Pour cream mixture over them. Cover with plastic wrap and refrigerate to cool.

Yield: 3 large or 6 small servings.

- -

As a Gift: Remove plastic wrap and place a mandarin orange segment and fresh mint leaf atop each cup of custard. Bundle separately in clear gift wrap and tie with a ribbon. Add instruction: *Keep refrigerated until ready to serve.*

Honey Butter

2 sticks salted butter, room
temperature

½ cup liquid honey

Blend butter and honey together until smooth.
Does not require refrigeration.

. . . .

As a Gift: Present in a pretty antique butter crock with a good lid.
Bundle all in clear plastic wrap and tie a small butter knife into the bow.
Or use a small canning jar with topper and ribbon tied at the neck.

Fruit and Nut Jumble

1 pound package unsalted
 mixed nuts
1 pound bag diced mixed, dried
 fruit

½ cup sweetened flaked coconut,
 toasted

Chop nuts to match diced fruit in size. Add fruit and coconut.
Store in container with tight lid.

Yield: 3 cups.

As a Gift: Present this healthy, colorful mix in clear, cellophane bags with
tented labels stapled to the top. Hole punch for a ribbon. Include the
serving suggestion: *Serve over ice cream or hot cereal.*

Artichoke Salad Dressing

1 (8 ounce) container artichoke
   cheese dip
½ cup ranch dressing

½ cup half-and-half
¼ teaspoon paprika
¼ teaspoon celery salt

Combine cheese dip, ranch dressing, half-and-half, paprika, and celery salt. Mix well and serve with crisp green salad. Refrigerate.

Yield: 1½ cups.

As a Gift: Present in small lidded glass canning jar. (No sealing is necessary.) Stand the jar in a pretty small dressing bowl with matching dipper or spoon. Bundle all in cellophane wrap and tie with a bow. Attach a sticky label to the jar that includes the name of the dressing and the instruction: *Keep refrigerated.* A very elegant salad dressing for a busy hostess!

Notes

Notes

Notes

Notes

Notes

Notes

Notes

Notes

Index